JOURNEYS AND STORIES

PORTUGAL

MAINLAND

A JOURNEY THROUGH MAINLAND PORTUGAL

INTRODUCTION	4
ENTRE DOURO AND MINHO	6
Viana do Castelo	8
Caminha	11
Ponte de Lima	12
Barcelos	13
Braga	14
Gerês	16
Guimarães	17
Porto	20
Vila Nova de Gaia	34
Póvoa de Varzim and Vila do Conde	36
Amarante	37
TRÁS-OS-MONTES E ALTO DOURO	38
Vila Real	40
Chaves	41
Bragança	42
Douro	44
Lamego	48
Peso da Régua	49
Vila Nova de Foz Côa	50
Miranda do Douro	51
BEIRA LITORAL	52
Santa Maria da Feira	54
Arouca	55
Aveiro	56
Ílhavo	59
Viseu	60
Coimbra	62
Conímbriga	65
Buçaco	66
BEIRA INTERIOR	68
Serra da Estrela	70
Guarda	72
Seia	74
Covilhã	75
Castelo Branco	76
Monsanto, Idanha-a-Nova	77
ESTREMADURA AND RIBATEJO	78
Leiria	80
Caldas da Rainha	81
Fátima	84
Alcobaça	86
Nazaré	87
São Martinho do Porto	88
Peniche	89
Grutas de Mira de Aire	90
Batalha	91
Óbidos	92
Santarém	94
Castelo de Almourol	95
Tomar	96
LISBON AND SETÚBAL	98
Mafra	100
Queluz	101
Sintra	102
Lisbon	106
Cascais	126
Setúbal	128
Palmela	129
Sesimbra	130
Arrábida	131
ALENTEJO	132
Estremoz	134
Vila Viçosa	135
Arraiolos	136
Elvas	137
Portalegre	138
Marvão	139
Alqueva	140
Monsaraz	141
Beja	142
Évora	144
Southwest Alentejo Natural Park and Vicentina Coast	147
ALGARVE	148
Aljezur	150
Sagres	151
Silves	152
Lagos	153
Portimão	154
Albufeira	155
Faro	156
Vilamoura	158
Tavira	159
CREDITS	160

MARIA EMMANVELS VI
CATHOLICORVM ECVM F...

LEONE   A.MANTA

Introduction

Portugal is one of the oldest countries in Europe, having kept the same borders for more than 800 years. Its history is mirrored in the countless prehistoric, Roman, Celtic and Middle Age remains.

Geographically, Portugal is located in the most Western part of Europe and has a large coastline, which was advantageous during the Period of the Discoveries. The Portuguese played a predominant role in this "great village" and were pioneers in globalisation.

It is also one of the most southern countries where sunlight teases the land, attracting many visitors from more northern countries looking for a place in the sun.

Portugal is also one of the countries with the largest number of UNESCO World Heritage sites as well as being one of the rare countries which receive more visitors than the total number of its inhabitants.

The cultural and geographical diversity of the country is huge: from the fresh green countryside of the Minho and the Douro, with their Celtic heritage, to the dry baking plains of the Alentejo and the Algarve, flavoured with their Moorish influences. The country possesses many facets, like an intricately embroidered blanket. This diversity is reflected in its wines, with the country's various demarcated regions, each with their own specific characteristics, which offer you some of the most distinct and unique wines in the World.

It has a bountiful coastline, with plenty of beaches with fine sand and giant waves, and a blue and emerald sea and golden cliffs. The Algarve beaches are the most sought after and are amongst the best in the world.

So this is Portugal: a mosaic of hand painted multi-coloured tiles. A mosaic of contrasts containing fishermen and shepherds, cool and warm, green and dry countryside, mountains and plains, snow and beach, granite, schist and lime, castles and contemporary buildings, tradition and modernity. To sum up, Portugal is like its wines: *multifaceted*. However, there is a common thread running through all this diversity: the warmth and friendliness of its people. Just like the aftertaste of a good wine that lasts and lasts.

Pedro Rodrigues

Embroidered Love

It was a slow afternoon, like those which come to warn us that time is something we must respect. Time doesn't always pass at the rhythm we want it to, and I had to study for a faculty test, but something impelled me towards inattention.

My mother knocked on the door, thus taking me out of that state in which I almost drown myself in a river of thoughts that constantly brought me back his image, in an uncontrollable swirl. She asked me, with a sweet voice, if she could interrupt, while I was immersed in a book. She had a box in her hand to show me.

I had already seen several 'lovers' handkerchiefs' for sale at the handicraft shops, but I had never paid them much attention. My hands took that small square of embroided cloth that laid, timeless, in its box.

My mother explained that that handkerchief had been embroidered by her grandmother: "Back then relationships were not like the ones from today... Your great-grandmother used to sew next to the window. One day, she noticed that a small pebble had slightly dashed against the window. She took a peep and saw at a glance a boy who fascinated her with his charming smile. After that, the boy kept passing there, in the evenings. Sometimes he threw her a flower, a shell or a colourful pebble; other times he just walked slowly and whistled. Until, one day, she surprised him, throwing him this handkerchief, which he started to wear around his neck. At that moment, both their hearts were overflowed with joy, as they both knew they were getting married."

While my mother left the room, I stared at that handkerchief, kindly embroidered with hearts, keys and a dove with a letter on its beak. Almost without noticing it, I copied the quatrain embroided on the handkerchief on my notebook, avoiding the misspellings: "Here is my heart/ and the key to open its door/ I have nothing more to give you/ And you have nothing more to ask me for."

The simplicity and the purity of those gestures and that love showed me what I didn't want to see before. I forgot the slowness of time, I erased his cell phone number and I smiled again.

Susana Fonseca

Panoramic view of Viana do Castelo

Viana Cultural Centre

Viana do Castelo Municipal Library

Parish Church

← *Pages 6 / 7. D. Luís I bridge seen from the Serra do Pilar viewpoint*

Fountain at Praça da República

Viana do Castelo is a city with a unique beauty and one of its *ex libris* is, without a doubt, the Basilica or Temple of the Sacred Heart of Jesus, better known as Temple of Santa Luzia. The interior of this monument has its inspiration in the Sacré-Coeur Basilica, in Montmartre, Paris. This amazing temple is located at the top of the Santa Luzia hill, where one is presented with an astonishing view over the region, which combines sea, river [the Lima] and a large mountain complex. A place where our eyes are moved by such beauty.

In the middle of the city, we find a Fountain at Praça da República. It is a Renaissance work, from the authorship of the quarryman from Porto, João Lopes, located at the eastern side of the square - in front of the former City Hall. Among the vast natural, cultural and architectonic heritage of Viana do Castelo, there is still to mention the Eiffel Bridge, from the authorship of Gustave Eiffel. Inaugurated in June 30th of 1878, it is an exemplar of the Cast-Iron Architecture.

Railway station

Pilgrimage of Nossa Senhora d'Agonia (Zés-pereiras)

On the municipality of **Viana do Castelo** there are about 70 celebrations and pilgrimages per year, from which we highlight the Festivities of Nossa Senhora D'Agonia, in August, which attract thousands of tourists from all over the world. Since the 20th till the next weekend, Viana is filled with colours and joy and, in the streets, one can see bagpipers, *Zés-pereiras* [large drum players], *gigantones* and *cabeçudos* [giant human figures with large heads]. By the morning of the 20th, the procession till the sea takes place. However, it is the march of the major-domos that officially opens the festivities, with thousands of local women dressed with their traditional costumes and wearing lots of gold around their neck. The high point of the festivities is the Historical and Ethnographic Parade, during which one can see the allegorical floats. On the last day it takes place the Costume Party, where women wear their laced outfits, representative of the country and city life. To enhance the beauty of the parade, also join it the women with their black velvet and satin dresses. The scarves with which they cover their heads are of natural silk and the socks are of white cotton. The gold and the sparkling glass beads are part of the costume. The nights are lighted by the cascade fireworks, falling from the bridge and lighting up the city sky.

Nossa Senhora d'Agonia

Fishing boat at River Minho

Fountain at Largo do Terreiro

Parish Church

On the northern of Portugal, it is located the municipality of **Caminha**, at about 25 km from Viana do Castelo. The visitors are presented with a miscellany of vegetation, magnificent beaches, hills and rivers - Minho, Couro and Âncora. In Caminha, we recommend a visit to the Mother Church, as well as to the Clock Tower where one can get to know the historical centre better. One of the striking places is the Ínsua, a rocky islet which divides the River Minho mouth. There, one can find the ruins of a convent, a church and a lighthouse, all surrounded by a fortress.

There are several handicraft sellers on this region, giving it an atmosphere of authenticity.
Some of the region's typical dishes are the Fish stew, the Lamprey rice or the Dry flounders from Lanhelas. The offer is also varied in what concerns confectionery. You may enjoy a walk through the walking trails or a kayak ride and practice nautical ski or scuba diving.

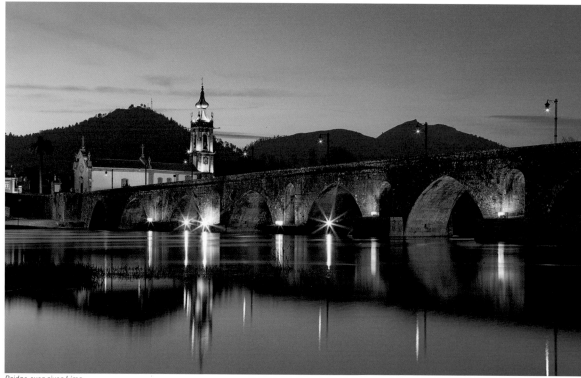

Bridge over river Lima

Local tradition of Vaca das Cordas

Praça de Camões

Ponte de Lima, Portugal's oldest village, is located by River Lima, which thus gave its name to it.

The most famous postcard of the city is the one with the bridge over the river, an authentic work of art, which combines medieval and roman styles. On the bridge line there is the historical centre, where one can find the *Torre da Cadeia* [Prison Tower] which proves that this village used to be a small citadel surrounded by walls. Currently, *Torre da Cadeia* hosts the Tourism Office. Ponte de Lima is also known by the fairs and festivals, such as the Horse Fair, taking place in June or July, and the International Garden Festival, which takes place every year from May to October. The so-called *Feiras Novas* are the municipality's most famous celebrations, during which you can watch the *concertina toccatas*, the music band concerts, the livestock contests and the parades. *Vaca das Cordas* is a famous tradition in the region, taking place in June, by the evening. The cow, or currently the wild bull, starts the race in front of the gate of Nossa Senhora de Aurora, in the middle of the historical centre. The animal is then guided till the Mother Church, and it should run around it three times, respecting the tradition.

Church of Bom Jesus da Cruz

Palace of the Counts of Barcelos

Barcelos Medieval bridge

Roosters of Barcelos

Barcelos, a city with millenary roots, is rich in heritage, legends and traditions. The most famous legend is associated with the Rooster, which may have served as a proof of innocence to a man, unfairly accused. The Cross of Senhor do Galo, located in front of the city's Mother Church, is also connected to the same legend. Over time, the roosters became one of Portugal's trademarks, being possible to find them in handicraft shops and in the weekly Fair of Barcelos. In the city's historical centre there are several monuments, among which the Palace of the Counts of Barcelos, where the Archaeology Museum is installed.

Stairway and Sanctuary of Bom Jesus do Monte

Church of Bom Jesus

Sanctuary of Our Lady of Sameiro

The Sanctuary of Bom Jesus do Monte, or **Sanctuary of Bom Jesus de Braga**, is a religious and touristic place, located in Tenões, a parish in Braga. The lush wood involving this Sanctuary grants it beauty and mysticism. The stairways, flanked by the centuries-old trees, take the walker to successive chapels, which represent passages from the Passion of Christ. In the middle of the way up, there is a viewpoint from which the city can be seen. Then, the space becomes wider and one can see, at the top, the Church of Bom Jesus.

The **Sanctuary of Our Lady of Sameiro** is a Marian sanctuary dating from the early 20th century, located about 3 km from Bom Jesus Sanctuary. It is one of most visited Marian shrines, second only to the Sanctuary of Fátima. Inside, note the main altar made of granite and the silver sacrarium. Outside the church you cannot miss the monumental stairs, topped with the images of the Virgin Mary and the Sacred Heart of Jesus. In 1982 it was visited by Saint John Paul II, whose sculpture stands at the bottom of the stairs.

Cathedral of Braga

Garden of Santa Bárbara

Arco da Porta Nova

Praça da República

The city of **Braga**, named *Bracara Augusta* by the Romans, has more than 2000 years of history. In the year of 1070, D. Pedro, the first Bishop of Braga, has organised the Diocese, driving the city's development. The urban area has grown around the Cathedral. In an environment of religious fervour, were built, throughout the centuries, monasteries, convents and churches. The city still preserves the prestige of country's religious capital. One manifestation of that is the fact that its streets get filled with candles and people watching the majestic processions, during the Holy Week. Besides the *Arco da Porta Nova*, the city's entry door, Braga is also known by the splendid houses of the 18th century, its gardens and its parks. The garden of Santa Bárbara, for example, is located next to the Medieval wing of Braga's Episcopal Palace. The Cathedral, located on one of the World's oldest Christian cities, is considered a centre of episcopal diffusion. It is an important temple of the Portuguese Romanesque, although having other architectonic styles. There one can find the Cathedral of Braga Treasure-Museum, containing assets with inestimable value, having works within a period of 1500 years, synthesising Christian life.

Oak grove at Mata da Albergaria

About 40 years ago the first National Park was created. With an area of over 72 thousand hectares, the Peneda Gerês National Park comprehends the municipalities of Melgaço, Arcos de Valdevez, Ponte da Barca, Terras do Bouro and Montalegre, and the mountains of Peneda, Soajo, Amarela, Gerês, as well as the uplands of Laboreiro and Mourela. The forest, even though being dominated by the oak trees, is quite diversified, being also found there sorts such as the holy, the *azereiro (Prunus lusitanica)*, the birch, the pine tree and the strawberry tree. This Park has several attractions, but the natural lagoons and *Mata da Albergaria* are definitely the most sought. The *spas* of Gerês are also famous in Portugal for the therapeutic qualities of their waters.

Mizarela Bridge

Castle of Guimarães

Palace of the Dukes of Bragança

Vila Flor Cultural Centre

Panoramic view of Praça da Oliveira

Largo do Toural

"Here was born Portugal"

Being called "Cradle City", **Guimarães** has a prominent place on the History of Portugal, as it was in this city that Portugal was born as a nation. In fact, according to tradition, here was probably born the first King of Portugal, D. Afonso Henriques.

The historical centre, today classified World Heritage, sends us back to the time of the foundation of the Portuguese nationality, as reminds us the sign "Here was born Portugal", on one of the wall's tower. The Castle and the Chapel of São Miguel, where D. Afonso Henriques was probably baptized, are part of the intramural area. You may also visit the Church of Nossa Senhora da Oliveira, rebuilt in honour of the Virgin Mary after the victory in the Battle of Aljubarrota, and the *Padrão do Salado*, edified in appreciation for the victory in the battle with the same name.

Praça de Santiago

Praça da Oliveira

Rua de Santa Maria

In the same area, we highlight the Palace of the Dukes of Bragança, which dates from the 15th century and was partially converted into a museum. Among the vast exhibited assets, the visitors can admire art works, tapestry and furniture from the 17th and 18th centuries. Despite the marking historical presence, Guimarães knows how to combine past and modernity. In order to do so, it has invested in modern and cosy spaces, such as the City Park and the Vila Flor Cultural Centre. The latter resulted from the recovery of the former Palace with the same name and hosts several cultural events. We also recommend a cable car tour up to the Penha Sanctuary, from where you can admire Guimarães, chosen for European Capital of Culture 2012. Don't leave the "Cradle City" without tasting the typical Roasted Kid and the Pies of Guimarães.

Houses at the Ribeira near quay of Estiva

Cathedral and Pillory

Cathedral's nave

Silver altar

Altar of Nossa Senhora da Silva

The **Cathedral** is one of the most relevant monuments of the city. It is located on the heart of the historical centre and rises itself on the landscape as an eye catalysing icon, welcoming the visitors. The historic testimonies seem to point out the existence of a previous construction, of religious nature, more humble, on the location of the current temple. The beginning of the Cathedral's construction, in a Romanesque style, dates back from the 12th century. At that time, the episcopal borough was organised according to the cathedral's function.

On its surrounding there was a set of streets, narrow lanes, small squares and alleys. In 1387, the Cathedral was embellished to celebrate the wedding of the King D. João I to the English princess Philippa of Lancaster (reinforcing the Anglo-Portuguese Alliance).

On the north side of the tower there is a bas-relief which represents a boat from the 14th century (a "coca"), symbolizing the maritime vocation of the city. The Cathedral's exterior has suffered significant alterations on the Baroque and Gothic periods. On its interior, one can highlight the sacristy, the João Gordo's chapel and the silver altar of the Blessed Sacrament.

Praça da Ribeira

Bairro da Sé

The **Ribeira** is one of the oldest and most attractive locations in Porto. It lies along the River Douro and forms part of the historical city centre, which is classified as a UNESCO World Heritage Site. In the early fifteenth century, the Ribeira was crowded with people connected to the river and the sea. The *Praça da Ribeira* was the meeting point for the merchants and the burghers. Nowadays the area is much frequented by tourists, with its various terraces and handicraft shops. The houses of Ribeira form a unique group, illustrating many a postcard of the city, to be relived in the eyes of its visitors.

Between Ribeira and the Cathedral the urban fabric of the city emerged with the appearance of houses, the streets, staircases and alleys such as *Rua da Lada*, *Rua da Reboleira*, *Rua dos Banhos* and the *Rua* and *Travessa do Barredo*. Walking along these streets means you can live and feel the history of Porto. Along *Rua da Reboleira* you will find examples of architecture from the late Middle Ages. The tower house at No. 59 retains its original structure.

Bairro de Miragaia

Rabelo boats

Regatta of Rabelo boats

The **rabelo sailboat** is a Portuguese seagoing vessel which is characteristic of the River Douro, where it traditionally carried the Port Wine from the Alto Douro to Vila Nova de Gaia, where the wine was stored, aged, bottled and marketed. The traditional rabelo sailboat is between 19 and 23 metres in length. Its construction, designated as clinker-built, is a perfect symbiosis of Nordic, Mediterranean and Oriental techniques adapted to a particular river and a particular activity. The boat was crewed by 6 or 7 men, who used a long oar over the stern to steer the boat.

With the implementation of the hydroelectric use of the river, the rabelo sailboats stopped being used in 1961. Currently, they are a tourist attraction in the River Douro, especially when they form part of the famous São João Regatta.

Photos from the collection of the Instituto dos Vinhos do Douro e do Porto

Port Wine is produced from grapes which come from the Demarcated and Regulated Douro Region, World Heritage Site, located about 100 km from Porto. Despite being produced with Douro's grapes and stored in the cellars of Vila Nova de Gaia, this drink became known as "Port Wine" since the second half of the 17th century, as it was exported from this town to the four corners of the world.

One of the characteristics which make Port Wine different from other wines is the fact that its fermentation is not finished, due to the addition of a neutral grape spirit. Port is naturally sweet and stronger than other wines.

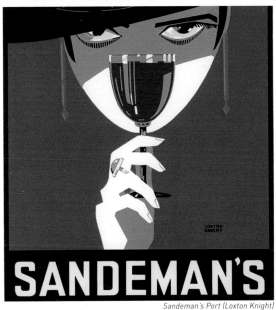

Sandeman's Port (Loxton Knight)

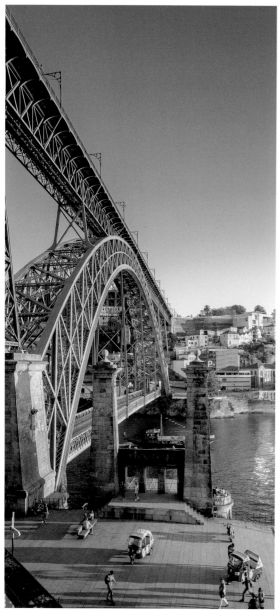

D. Luís I bridge

Arrábida bridge

São João bridge

Freixo bridge

D. Maria Pia bridge

The city of Porto is also known for its bridges, which cross the River Douro and connect to the city of Vila Nova de Gaia. They all have different characteristics and beautify the river: "The Dona Maria Pia bridge; the Dom Luís I bridge; the Arrábida bridge; the São João bridge, the Freixo bridge and the Infante bridge."

Panoramic view of Avenida dos Aliados

Detail from a building in granite

Porto's City Hall

To walk by **Avenida dos Aliados** is to feel the beat of the city with all its magnificence, which comes from the beautiful façades, the wide walkways, the building of the City Hall, the statues of different periods and, fundamentally, from the people who enliven this avenue, where the major events of the city are celebrated. Located downtown, it is a place to go ideally on foot. The buildings are made of granite, but present different characteristics which surprise us with the feeling of travelling back in time. Nowadays, some buildings belonging to bank entities share their space with several coffee shops and esplanades, trade stores and kiosks.

The avenue axis is paved with granite parallelepipeds. In 2006, it suffered a complete makeover planned by the architects Álvaro Siza Vieira and Eduardo Souto de Moura.

Aerial view of Porto and river Douro

Clérigos tower and tramway

Interior of Clérigos Church

Lello Bookshop

Built in the eighteenth century, the **Torre dos Clérigos**, designed by the architect Nicolau Nasoni, is an icon of the city of Porto. The church is part of the monument with the same name. With a height of 75 metres and containing six floors, this tower is one of the highest in Portugal. A climb to the top floor is rewarded with a spectacular view over the city and the River Douro.

Renowned internationally, **Lello Bookshop** is one of the most beautiful in the world. In addition to the architectural beauty of its exterior, in the neo-Gothic style, it is also captivating thanks to its cosy atmosphere. This bookshop has an extremely broad range of books, particularly Porrtuguese writers in various languages and foreign publication. The staircase and the stained glass window in the ceilingare its most iconic features.

São Bento train station

Built in the early twentieth century, the **São Bento Railway station** is one of the most visited railway stations in Portugal. Its façade is impressive and the atrium is lined with twenty thousand tiles, which depict various scenes from Portugal's history and the history of transportation.

The **Crystal Palace** owes its name to the beautiful iron and glass building which once existed there. Now you can check out the Sports Pavilion and its surroundings with flower beds, an aromatic garden, the avenue of Lime trees and the Almeida Garrett library, among the other agreeable locations. Due to its location, be sure to take advantage of the fantastic view over the river and the mouth of the Douro.

The **Stock Exchange Palace** is owned by the Porto Commercial Association. It has an imposing granite façade in the Neoclassical style. Each room has different features and is worth a guided tour. Of particular note are the wonderful Arabian Room and the Patio of Nations.

Crystal Palace

Stock Exchange Palace

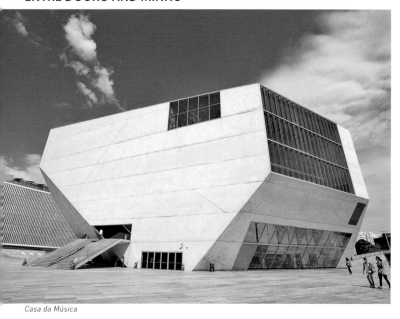

The interiors of Casa da Música

Casa da Música

Casa da Música, Sala Suggia

The **Casa da Música** is an icon of the city and was designed by the architect Rem Koolhaas to mark Porto being the European Capital of Culture. The building, shaped like a diamond, certainly does not go unnoticed due to its singular architecture. It contains two auditoriums and various areas for activities related to music. The interior spaces are amazing and worthy of a guided tour.

The **Serralves Foundation** comprises the park, villa and Museum of Contemporary Art. It is a cultural centre that promotes a variety of activities and which curates international exhibitions. The gardens of the park, with their beautiful panoply of trees and flowers, are an ideal place for taking a stroll. The Serralves Villa hosts temporary exhibitions.

Liquidambars' alley

Serralves villa

Serralves Museum

Fireworks at the D. Luís I bridge

São João do Porto is a traditional and unique celebration, in which the odour of grilled sardines invades the typical houses, and the sky magically fills with small hot air balloons. The revellers, armed with leeks and plastic hammers, walk joyfully for miles.

In several neighbourhoods, such as Fontaínhas, Massarelos or Miragaia, there are small festivals with folk singers and enthusiastic dancers.

The cascades and ornaments allusive to São João are a source of pride for the neighbourhoods' inhabitants, who on that night have dinner outside and offer sardines to whoever walks by.

It's a Catholic celebration, with a strong profane component, which is celebrated on the night from the 23rd to the 24th of June and which marks the birth of St. John the Baptist. It is certainly the longest night of the city, where the rule is to walk through neighbourhoods and festivals - since Passeio Alegre till Fontaínhas, passing through Ribeira, where at midnight, one can watch the fireworks. Thousands of people go to the *Invicta* to watch and participate in the city's main celebration. For many, the night ends at the beach with the sun already shinning.

Popular dance near Porto's cathedral

Port wine cellars

Port wine, from left to the right: Tawny, Ruby and White

It is on the riverside of **Vila Nova de Gaia** where one can find the cellars where the famous Port Wine ages, coming from the Douro terraces. Visiting their interior is an unforgettable experience. It is also recommendable to walk by the bank of River Douro on the so called *Cais de Gaia*, which has a dazzling view of Porto's *Ribeira*. However, there is much more to see and enjoy in Gaia. For instance, the Biological Park and the Santo Inácio Zoo deserve a visit due to the diversity of animals one can find there.

To those who enjoy outdoor sports, the Lavandeira Park is a good option, and to those who prefer the sea, Gaia offers a coastline with over 15 km long. If you choose to visit the city's historical centre, it is worth to go up to *Serra do Pilar* – a World Heritage Site - where one can now go using the cable car that connects it with the riverside area.

Port wine cellars

Porto's subway and Serra do Pilar

Cais de Gaia (Quay of Gaia)

Harbour of Póvoa de Varzim

Tile panels

A city with contemporary features, but also with older quarters, **Póvoa do Varzim** offers a rich and diverse fish-based cuisine. It has beautiful beaches, which makes it very popular in the summer. Its connection to the sea is represented in its tile panels - true works of art that depict the daily life of the fishermen. *Avenida dos Banhos* offers you discos, bars and terrace cafés. The casino is another of the city's attractions.

Vila do Conde is rich in cultural and architectural heritage and is a city known for its fishing harbour and beautiful beaches. The aqueduct at the entrance to the city provides our first surprise, and originally consisted of 999 arches. Noteworthy also is the 16th century carrack (*Nau Quinhentista*) and the *Forte de São João*. *Caxinas* is an area mainly devoted to activities related to fishing. This city is also known for its famous Bobbin lace.

The riverside area, 16th century carrak and Santa Clara Convent

Fort of São João Baptista

Aqueduct of Vila do Conde

Church and bridge of São Gonçalo over River Tâmega

Monastery of São Gonçalo

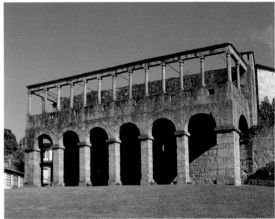

Magalhães' Manor House

What most characterizes the city of **Amarante** is, without a doubt, its historical centre, where one can appreciate, among other buildings, the São Gonçalo Bridge, over River Tâmega, and the Monastery of São Gonçalo. If we let ourselves be embraced by this landscape, we will get the feeling that it greets us with a mixture of romanticism and spirituality. Passing the bridge and entering the church, we perceive the existing devotion to Saint Gonçalo. One of the statues of the Saint is at the sacristy. The popular wisdom attests that whoever has the wish to get married should pull the rope located around the statue and make the request.

We recommend a visit to the Museum of the painter Amadeo de Souza-Cardoso, located near the monastery. Next, we suggest a walk by the margins of River Tâmega or through the city's picturesque streets, where you will be able to see what is left of the Magalhães' Manor House, a building from the 18th century, as well as to find bakeries with dainty traditional delicacies.

Another point of interest in this municipality is the Casa de Pascoaes, located in the parish of Gatão, where the Portuguese poet Teixeira de Pascoaes lived.

The Embrace of the Sun

I arrived in this country of saudade with an almost empty backpack. I checked-in, followed a path of agitated clouds, left the sweat of work marked on a grey seat and followed the direction, as planned, along a waterway to the Douro Valley I had heard about. I was curious about what I would find, since a couple of friends came to this region so often and repeated so many times that I too should come here.

One day, after leaving the alarm on, I made my way to work, as always. I saw all my e-mails and booked my trip with an online agency.

Now that I heard the guide's descriptions of the oldest demarcated and regulated wine-growing region in the world, I felt much lighter, absorbing more and more the green landscape mixed with gold.

I arrived here reinvigorated, I see myself reflected in the faces of the smiling children who run after their mothers, despite the hot air that invited them to rest. I lean back into a shadow to listen to the sources of light shining on the earth and the shale, making it ideal to receive the product of the arduous work of these people that seem to know how to live in a profound calm, without any thought to torment them, although a more attentive look will notice that it isn't quite like that. The concerns are also there, within the most loaded stares.

And I still have a lot to do and visit during this trip. In my notepad, there are some places not to be missed, recommended by my friends: a visit to a farm to try the nectar that is produced here, a trip on a historical train, a visit to the village of Ucanha, and many other wine-growing villages that I am keen to get to know.

At this time everything seems bigger than me, and the embrace of this landscape is so tender and warm that it makes me remember by mother's embraces.

Susana Fonseca

Vila Real City Hall

Pillory's Square

Casa de Mateus main façade

Vila Real is the district capital and was once the capital of the Trás-os-Montes province. Nowadays, one of the important focal points of the region is the University of Trás-os-Montes e Alto Douro, which attracts students to the city. The street circuit for racing cars in Vila Real is considered one of the best in Europe, and is held every year.

In the city centre, we recommend a stroll through the typical streets, where you can enjoy the regional cuisine and traditional confectionery.

Near the city, you can visit the Alvão Natural Park, where you can find the waterfalls of Fisgas of Ermelo and enjoy the plants and animals which are typical of the Park. Still in Alvão, you should visit the villages of Vila Marim and Lamas de Olo.

Casa de Mateus is a baroque-style building constructed during the 18th century under the supervision of the architect Nicolau Nasoni. In 1970, the Casa de Mateus Foundation was founded with the aim of preserving the house, studying its archives and promoting cultural, scientific and educational activities. The Foundation promotes various activities such as concerts, seminars, courses and exhibitions.

At Casa de Mateus it is possible to enter its rooms, which are richly decorated and furnished in the style of the period, the chapel and the magnificent gardens, lovingly cared for. Casa de Mateus produces sweets and wine marketed by Lavradores de Feitoria.

← Pages 38 / 39. River Douro

Roman bridge over River Tâmega

Chaves has a unique natural beauty, and several places worthy of visiting, such as the historical centre, from where it stands out the *Praça Camões*. With a strong religious nature, this municipality presents a wide range of temples one shouldn't miss. Other points of interest are, for example, the Roman Bridge; the Região Flaviense Museum; or even the Convent of the Ordem de Nossa Sra. da Conceição. Widely known is the *Spa* of Chaves and the Vidago Palace Hotel, one of the most luxurious hotels in the country. Gastronomically, one can highlight the sausages and the cured meats. Handicraft is also worthy of appreciation, namely for the black pottery, the basketry of Vilar de Nantes and the blankets of Soutelo.

Castle of Chaves

Vidago Palace

Castle of Bragança

Centre of Bragança

Domus Municipalis

Bragança is a municipality rich in traditions, and there are plenty of reasons to visit it. Two of the strongest traditions are the *Festas dos Rapazes* and the *Festa dos Caretos* [masks made of wood, leather, tinplate and cork]. The Caretos of Podence, in the municipality of Macedo de Cavaleiros, deserve to be highlighted. These representations of diabolic images go out to the streets, during the carnival festivities, with their cowbells on the colourful fringes of thick blankets.

Bragança is known for its handicraft, a very important activity in the region, and for its gastronomy, whose delicacies must be degusted by all visitors. To those who appreciate natural landscapes, we recommend a visit to the Montesinho Natural Park, which has diverse accommodation, sports and leisure services, perfect for a holiday period in contact with nature. For a longer walk, it is worth visiting the Citadel and all its surroundings, where one can find the *Portas da Vila* (Village Entrance), the castle walls, the Keep, the *Domus Municipalis* and the Pillory.

← *Page 42. 01- Castle of Bragança | 02- Caretos of Podence*

Aerial view of the Douro

Grape treading at Quinta do Vesúvio

Grape harvest at Quinta Nova de Nossa Senhora do Carmo

Blossoming Almond Tree

Quinta do Seixo

Boat trip on the River Douro

Bunch of red grapes

With a unique and dazzling landscape, the **Upper Douro** wine region is one of the places considered World Heritage, by UNESCO. There are several reasons for us to explore this magnificent region, but the most important one is the desire of discovering the land where the famous wine is produced. This nectar, named Port Wine after the 17th century, grows and ripens on the terraces of the Douro valleys.

Douro was the World's first demarcated and regulated wine region and it is divided into three main regions, different in geography and climate: Baixo Corgo, Cima Corgo and Upper Douro.

To enjoy the magnificent landscaping, you can follow the River Douro course on a train journey or on a cruise. The several *Quintas* (farms) of the region offer you the opportunity of participating, at the harvest season, in the grape harvest and in the works at the *lagares* (mills).

→ Page 47. 01- Quinta de Ventozelo and the village of Pinhão
02- Train at the bridge over the Tua river junction with the River Douro

General city overview

Cathedral of Lamego

Lamego is a monumental city, highlights of its architectural heritage being the Castle, the Cathedral and the Sanctuary and Stairway of Nossa Senhora dos Remédios. In addition to these monuments, there are various churches, houses with coat of arms, fountains and stone crosses that demonstrate the historical and religious importance that the municipality held and continues to hold over the region. Lamego was able to harmonise its history with development and the nature that surrounds it and constitutes one of the locations with a wide choice of hotels in the Douro region.

Sanctuary and Stairway of Nossa Senhora dos Remédios

River Douro and Peso da Régua

Panoramic view of Régua

Peso da Régua is a renowned and emblematic city of the region. With a history dating back to the Roman invasions, the city has modernized and become the centre of the Douro Railway between Porto and Pocinho. In 1756, after the Marquis of Pombal's decision to demarcate the Douro Region, Régua became recognized as the great trading post for Port Wine. There are now various vessels that take tourists on river cruises from Régua river dock. There is a wide range of hotels and visitors can taste the regional cuisine in one of the various restaurants. One of the must-see places is the Douro Museum, whose headquarters was installed, after upgrading works, in the former Company building in 2008.

Sunset landscape in Trás-os-Montes

Freixo de Numão Castle

River Douro

The city of **Vila Nova de Foz Côa** is located in a region called the warm land, due to the Mediterranean micro-climate that the municipality enjoys, allowing trees such as the fig, olive, orange and almond to be grown. The latter fill the landscapes of Foz Côa with fantastic flowers. Vale do Côa Archaeological Park is an authentic living museum, exhibiting the most important open-air paleolithic rock art site in the world. This place was designated World Heritage in 1998 by UNESCO.
We also draw your attention to the locations of Castelo Melhor, Almendra and Freixo de Numão.

Viewpoint at Castro de Vale da Águia, Miranda do Douro

Episcopal Palace

The origins of **Miranda do Douro** date back a long way, and it progressively became the most important fortified town in Trás-os-Montes. The municipality possesses a valuable cultural heritage spread over the different parishes, which continue to preserve part of their culture and popular traditions.

On the Miranda high plain, winter solstice festivals are still celebrated today, with rituals of profound mythological significance. In 1998, Mirandese officially became Portugal's second language. A large part of the municipality lives off agriculture and grazing, and the breeds Bovina Mirandesa, Churra Galega Mirandesa, Asinina Mirandesa and Cão de Gado Transmontano are native to the region. The spectacular cliffs of International Douro Natural Park are a highlight among the landscapes of the Mirandese plateau.

Sculpture by António Nobre: traditional costumes from Miranda do Douro

Salt Flower

I look for the silence and the freedom day after day, under the the sun, the rain or the wind. I am indifferent to the blasts' severity.

There are days when everything surrounds me. The past is made of ghosts who perch on these waters and come to talk with me about old days. We speak of the joy of coming to harvest the salt. We share stories about the families. A son who was born; a woman who recovered from a serious illness; an uncle who returned rich from Brazil; a kid who was the best at the school's exam and even a cat we got out of the roof without causing damages to the feline, or to the tiles. Stories from a past that no longer belongs to me.

My reality is the salt that I harvest from the salt pans - the salt flower, formed by the crystals which gather at the water's surface. If I don't harvest it on time and with care, it will settle at the bottom, becoming ordinary sea salt. Yesterday, when I got home, my youngest goddaughter was waiting for me at the door. She arrived from Porto to do a school project, and wanted me to take her to the city centre on Sunday. After long insisting and already with a tear in her eye, she gave up, but I cleaned her face, asking her not to waste the salt of her tears for so little.

When the day arrived, I took her to the centre. We took a ride on a BUGA, and walked along the canals. I showed her the moliceiros and its paintings. We went to a bakery and I offered her a Pipinha de Ovos-Moles, with some striped houses painted on it. She laughed, saying that they looked like houses in pyjamas. I've explained her that those houses were located at Costa Nova, and promised her that, one day, I would take her there; but, at that moment, I wanted to show her something of my life.

Back to the salt pans, where the tides drink water from the Ria, we remained between the silence and the world. I showed her the small mountains of white gold, essential to our life. At that place, everything fitted. I explained her that, in anywhere else, the sun could be seen from horizon to horizon. From those rectangles was harvested the salt, with wisdom and love. She felt the wind on her face and understood the liberty reflected on the waters. White tears emerged from her eyes.

Susana Fonseca

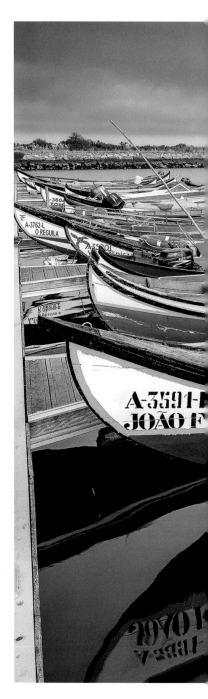

Castle of Santa Maria da Feira

Show of the "Imaginarius" festival

↑ ↗ ↙ Medieval Journey in the Land of Santa Maria

Santa Maria da Feira is a municipality with strong cultural traditions and knows how to bet on the promotion of the events that take place during the year. The Medieval Fair – one of the most important at a national level -; the *Imaginarius* - a single quality event on the performing arts area and one of the main references of Portugal's street theatre -; and the *Festa das Fogaceiras*, a secular tradition and the municipality's most emblematic festivity, are good examples. From the cultural buildings, the highlight goes to the truly amazing medieval castle and to the congress centre, the *Europarque*, which also plays host to an extensive and qualified cultural agenda.

← Pages 52 / 53. Bica Quay, Murtosa

Church of the Monastery of Arouca

Paiva Walkways

Church of the Monastery of Arouca

Of note in **Arouca** is the monastery where the blessed Mafalda of Portugal lived, who would have become Queen if her marriage had not been annulled. The female wing of the Cistercian monastery became the richest and largest of its order throughout the whole country. With the dissolution of the religious orders, the convent was to be stripped of its riches, but thanks to the population of Arouca, it has preserved much of its heritage. The conventual and manorial desserts have been handed down from generation to generation. Be sure to taste the *castanhas doces* (sweet chestnuts), the *roscas de amêndoa* (almond twists) and the *barrigas de freira* (nuns' bellies). Arouca is also known for its meat dishes, such as roast veal and its Alvarenga steaks. The Arouca Geopark is renowned for its exceptional geological heritage, particularly the *"pedras parideiras"* of Castanheira and the beautiful Mizarela waterfall in the Serra da Freita.

Panoramic view of the Ria

Cais do Botirão (quay of Botirão)

There are several cities which benefit from the privilege of being near watercourses. **Aveiro** is no exception, as it stands out thanks to its famous *Ria* (river branch), abundant in fish and waterbirds.

The *moliceiros,* unique boats with a simple decoration reminding the *naïf* painting, are also connected to the *Ria,* still collecting the seaweed - a great fertilizer for arid lands. Besides the *Ria* and its surroundings, Aveiro district also has beautiful beaches, namely the one of S. Jacinto. The architecture is a representative element of the city as well, being highlighted the façades in *Art Nouveau*.

For those who enjoy outdoor activities, one can choose to go on a tour on the *moliceiro*, ride a BUGA (free-use bicycles of Aveiro) or try one of the several nautical sports. As far as gastronomy is concerned, Aveiro is known for its fishermen dishes and, in confectionery, by the famous *ovos moles*, a sweet yellow paste delicacy.

Naïf painting of a moliceiro boat

Cultural and Congress Centre of Aveiro

Railway station

Harbour

Casa Major Pessoa - Art Nouveau Museum of Aveiro

A note on the University of Aveiro, established in 1973 and which rapidly became one of the most dynamic and innovative Portuguese universities. Its campus constitutes a 'mini-town' surrounded by the natural beauty of the salt pans (page 53), with a view of the *Ria*, and near the city centre. The institution is annually visited by hundreds of tourists who enjoy the singular architecture with buildings designed by the awarded architects Álvaro Siza Vieira and Eduardo Souto de Moura.

The guided tours to the Santiago da Fonte Salt Pit, property of University of Aveiro, allow the visitor to get to know this outdoor cultural landscape and the different types of artisanal salt which are here produced and extracted from. In addition, it also has a recovered warehouse with two purposes: supporting the salt production and developing scientific and didactic activities, promoting the accessible tourism as well.

"Palheiros", houses of Costa Nova

Barra's Lighthouse

Dunes at Barra Beach

Known for the porcelain industry *Vista Alegre*, the city of **Ílhavo** is also identified by the *Farol da Barra* - the highest of the 48 Portuguese maritime lighthouses, located in Barra, in the parish of Gafanha da Nazaré. Also famous is the extensive shore of the Costa Nova do Prado beach. Another attraction is the typical houses of this beach - the *Palheiros*. They are characterised for their wooden façades, striped with bright and joyful colours, alternated with white colour. As far as gastronomy is concerned, we recommend the bread of Vale de Ílhavo, made in an artisanal way and cooked on a wood oven.

Cathedral forecourt

The city of **Viseu** has been developing as a meeting and exchange point due to its central position in the country. Very much linked to the history and legends of the city is the figure of Viriato, the Lusitanian leader who protected Viseu from the Roman invaders. It is believed that the Cava do Viriato park would have been the location of the military field and the battles which took place. You can find a statue erected in honour of this warrior to be found on one of the many walking paths in this wooded area. One of the oldest monuments of the city, the thirteenth century Cathedral, stands imposingly in the centre of Viseu. It has a Mannerist façade with interior decoration in the Baroque style and it has three naves. The upper cloister houses the Museum of Sacred Art, which displays pieces from the Cathedral's collection: sculptures, furniture, safes and reliquaries, among other items. In front of the Cathedral stands the *Igreja da Misericórdia* (Church of Mercy), which was built in the eighteenth century. Of note is its splendid entrance and bell towers. Its interior includes Neoclassical altars and altarpieces in white and gold. There are also vestiges of medieval times to be admired, such as a section of the city wall – the *Porta do Soar*, which is the last of the seven original gates. Along the outer arc is the royal shield and an image of Saint Francis. Be sure to stroll down Rua D. Duarte, a street dedicated to commerce where you can see one of the most exuberant sixteenth century Manueline windows in the *Casa do Ducado*.

Cathedral

Statue of Viriato

Cathedral, cloisters

City main view and river Mondego

Santa Cruz Church

Students in academic costume

The city of **Coimbra** is surrounded by a mystical aura that leads to it having even more charm in its hour of farewell – or so the song goes. The hill where the University (World Cultural Heritage Site) now stands has previously been a Neolithic castra, a Roman town, a Visigoth settlement, Medina, capital of the *Reconquista*, and the royal city of the Afonso dynasty and a Manueline palace. Coimbra was the capital of the kingdom for two hundred years during the period of the first monarchs. The first king of Portugal, Dom Afonso Henriques, installed his court in the Royal Palace of Alcáçova in 1130. With the founding of the University, Coimbra became a more prominent place. The university was actually founded in Lisbon by Dom Dinis in 1290, and transferred to Coimbra in 1537, where it was located in the palace. On that date, Coimbra became a seat of higher education. University professors from the most educated countries were recruited. Of note within the visitable part of the university is the Hall of Great Acts *(Sala dos Capelos)*, which was the scene of

São Joanina Library

São Miguel Chapel

Sala dos Capelos (Hall of Great Acts)

major court ceremonies. In the meantime, the room has been made suitable for educational use, and houses public academic thesis defences and formal university ceremonies. The city has been the centre of student gatherings which, perhaps more due to the intellectual bohemia than the rigour of the classes, have provided the best cadres for the country. The Johannine library, recognized as the most sumptuous university library and a masterpiece of the European Baroque, was built between 1717 and 1728, under the aegis of Dom João V.

It is accessed through by a monumental entrance gate, like a triumphal arch. Inside, visitors will discover a succession of three large areas, leading the eye to focus on the portrait of the founding monarch. The interior is lined with shelves decorated in Chinese motifs on a green, red and black background. It is not hard to imagine the assembled students, studying at the furniture still present in the room.

Fado of Coimbra

Portugal dos Pequenitos

Botanical Garden

Coimbra Fado is linked to the academic traditions of the University. It is sung by men and both the *fadistas* (singers) and the musicians wear academic costume. It is sung at night in parks or in the streets of the city, particularly near the *Mosteiro da Sé Velha*. The fado is accompanied by a Portuguese guitar and a classical guitar. It is traditional to serenade the lady you wish to conquer outside her window. The most frequent themes are student loves, love for the city and other topics related to the human condition.

The **Botanical Garden**, which belonged to the School of Natural Philosophy, was created in 1773. Its lush vegetation reflects its botanical studies and exchanges with various countries.

Portugal dos Pequenitos (Portugal of the Little Ones) is an entertainment, pedagogic and tourist park which opened in 1940. It provides a miniature and detailed presentation of aspects of the architecture and history of Portugal. This fun theme park is one of the oldest in the world.

Cantaber house

Conímbriga is the name given to a set of Roman ruins that lie close to Vila de Condeixa. These are the largest remains of Roman civilization in Portugal. Conímbriga was a notable area and had a large settlement in the Iron Age, which was later romanized. The whole city was sacked in 468, with the houses being destroyed and many people imprisoned. Later, pasture covered the land and the ancient city disappeared. Archaeological exploration of the site began in the twentieth century, and was carried out by the University of Coimbra. The elements of the lower pavements survived the passage of time. The most numerous remains date from the 2nd to the 4th centuries. The collections exhibited in the museum provide a clearer picture of the Roman civilization. Roman houses had an area dedicated to family life, the decoration of which is especially interesting, and the rich polychrome mosaic is a well maintained example, proof of the refinement of this period at Conímbriga. Of particular note in the ruins is the House of the Fountains, the central garden of which has over 400 water spouts.

Mosaic detail

Casa dos Repuxos (House of the Fountains)

Vale dos fetos (Valley of ferns)

Detail of the centennial tree

Mata Nacional do Buçaco

Buçaco has a rich heritage of exceptional monuments. The site reminds us of the enchanted forests of childhood stories. Its core is made up of the Buçaco Palace Hotel - the former Royal Palace - and the convent of Santa Cruz alongside the hermitage, the chapels of devotion and the Steps that make up the *Via Sacra*. Of note also is the *Fonte Fria*, with its staircase, tanks and bellevues, especially that of the Cruz Alta, and its woodland. This is one of the richest forests in terms of architectural heritage, both from a cultural and natural point of view, with about 250 species of trees and shrubs, which can be divided into three groups: the Arboretum, the gardens and the Valley of Ferns and the Relic Forest. The biodiversity found in Buçaco expresses the uniqueness of this magical space. The forest belonged to the Bishopric of Coimbra until it was donated to the Order of the Discalced Carmelites in 1628, who remained there until the order was dissolved. The Buçaco Forest Foundation, which manages this patrimony, currently organizes various activities such as Sunday group visits to Buçaco, historical tours and Buçaco by moonlight, among others.

Buçaco Palace

Buçaco Palace

Staircase from the Buçaco Palace

Eternal Star

They had agreed on the places where they would make their stops on that first family outing. The parents and aunt and uncle were going with the children, and they were eager to show more of their country to the kids. It was with a joyful spirit that they left early in the morning and gathered together, before setting out on the long trip. It would be an adventure and a change to the day-to-day routine of home school and school home. They did not want to miss their ride for that journey.

In one of the following cars, there was a couple with their daughter. She had her eyes glued to the window. She knew they were going to Serra da Estrela and asked her mother if she could touch the star when they got there. Her mother tried to explain that this was not possible, but the girl thought her mother was hiding something important and asked her father the same question. She was then twice doubly unhappy with his answer. The father sighed and said he would tell her a story about the origin of the name of the mountain. Even though she was upset because all she wanted was the star, she listened to her father telling her about a kid who was a shepherd and lived alone in a village. He didn't have either a father or a mother? She interrupted. No. The father replied. Didn't he have any cousins or uncles or brothers? The father shrugged, already regretting that he had remembered the legend. No. He lived alone. The father repeated this and warned her to stop with her questions, otherwise he would not tell the story. Sulkily, the girl leaned back and looked out of the window again.

The boy lived alone in a village and in the distance, he used to see a star that shone more brightly than all the others. At one point he came to the conclusion that the star was calling to him. The boy said goodbye to his neighbours and told them he was going to look for the star. His neighbours told him not to do that, because the distance seemed much larger than he imagined it to be. The boy did not want to hear the warnings and set off on a starry night with his dog. He walked and walked and walked. From time to time, he stopped by the roadside to rest. He fed himself on fruits and roots and what he was able to catch with his catapult. He felt he was growing and sometimes looked at his reflection in a pool of water. One day the dog died. He buried it and kept walking towards the star. When he arrived, he was already an old man. The star, which had waited patiently for him, accompanied him and spoke with him. One day he came across a subject of the king who informed him that his master wanted to give him great wealth in exchange for the star. The old man did not accept the proposal. That night, the star shone even brighter and rewarded him with eternal life.

When the father looked in the rear-view mirror, the girl had already fallen asleep. She only woke up when they took a break for lunch. She told the story to her cousins and invented a happy ending for the boy who had not become old in her dreams.

Susana Fonseca

Sabugueiro village

Ski resort

On top of the Serra da Estrela

Serra da Estrela Cheese

← *Pages 68 / 69. Serra da Estrela*

Serra da Estrela

The **Serra da Estrela** is the highest mountain range in mainland Portugal, and forms part of the Serra da Estrela Natural Park. The main attractions of this park are its snow, flora and fauna, as well as the cultural, historical and culinary wealth of the region. The *Torre*, the highest marked point, is 1993 m above sea level.

You can enjoy the snow, and stay in a mountain resort during the winter. The Vodafone Ski Resort provides fun for everyone. Penhas da Saúde offers tourist accommodation and support for skiing. The Penhas Douradas resort overlooks the town of Manteigas.

You can also take part in cultural and environmental tourism. As for the former, there are routes which take in the Former Jewish Quarters, the Historic villages, the castles, the Discoverers and the Woolen Industry. As regard the latter, you can choose the Route of the Glacial Valleys, that of the 4 rivers, or that of the 25 Lakes and its natural areas.

The gastronomic highlight is the buttery cheese from *Serra da Estrela*, a truly gluttonous cheese when accompanied by a good wine. It is produced exclusively from sheep's milk from the region.

The Serra da Estrela watch dogs, which stem from the region, were used in the grazing of sheep. This native breed is known for its friendliness towards its owners and aggressivity towards strangers. Evidence of their bravery are the battles they formerly waged against wolf packs to save their flocks.

Castelo Rodrigo

Rock art from Penascosa Park, Foz Côa

D. Sancho I, Guarda

Guarda Cathedral

The city of **Guarda** is part of the mountainous landscape of the Serra da Estrela. It is located in a high strategic area close to Spain. The city owes its name to the fact that it served as a frontier guard.

It is usually known as the city of the 5 F's: *Forte* (Strong – because of its Castle and walls), *Farta* (Abundant - due to the fertility of the Mondego River), *Fria* (Cold – due to the snow from the Serra), *Fiel* (Loyal – due to its resistance) and *Formosa* (Beautiful – because of its mountain scenery). It is 1056 m above sea level, and is thus the highest city in the entire country.

The old town has many monuments that you can visit. We would highlight some sections of the wall and the 3 entrance gates that remain - the *Porta do Sol/da Erva*, that of *D'El Rei* and the *Ferreiros*. All that is left of the Castle now is the Keep, which affords a beautiful view over the city.

The Cathedral has a Romanesque, Gothic and Manueline style and was constructed during the 14th and 16th centuries. The exterior is decorated with gargoyles that evoke monsters, fantastic animals and scowls.

The Johannine Church of the Misericórdia, the Baroque church of S. Vicente, with an admirable tile panel, and the Jewish Quarter, are all worth a visit.

The village of Almeida is part of the district of Guarda and is a noteworthy feature on the horizon as it is surrounded by a defensive wall in the shape of 12-pointed star. It is an unusual example of military architecture. In the village you can be sure to find good food, especially game dishes.

Seia Town Hall

Seia, located on the southwest slope of the Serra da Estrela, is characterized by its variety of fauna and flora, delicious food and rich cultural traditions.

This town with medieval features was conquered from the Moors in 1132 by Dom Afonso Henriques. Among the various monuments that testify to its antiquity we would highlight its Mother Church where a castle once stood. You can also visit the Town Hall, a palatial eighteenth century building, the Chapel of Saint Pedro, with a Romanesque entrance porch from the thirteenth century; the Botelhos Manor House with its Manueline windows and the eighteenth-century church of Misericórdia.

Seia is also known for its Bread Museum, which showcases the history of baking bread and its ingredients, as well as the Toy Museum.

Seia also hosts the Interpretation Centre for the Serra da Estrela, where you can discover the history of the Serra and watch a 3D video that will take you on a virtual tour of the main features of the region.

Rural landscape

Santo André Stairs

Misericórdia church

The city of **Covilhã** is known for its woollen manu-facturing culture, which links it to the early history of Portugal. Of the castle, only a single rampart remains from where you can obtain a beautiful view of the city. Near the castle the free public elevator offers a way up one of the several steep hills of the city. The journey provides a beautiful panoramic view. If you prefer, you can opt for the Santo André stairs, which run alongside the elevator.

With regard to the monuments, you can visit the Baroque style *Igreja da Misericórdia* and the Igreja de *Santa Maria*, built in the 16th century, with a façade covered with tiles representing extracts from the life of the Virgin.

Church of Stª Maria Maior

Bishop's palace garden in Castelo Branco

Bishop's palace garden in Castelo Branco

São Miguel Church

Castle of the Order of the Templars

In **Castelo Branco** you can visit several monuments. From the castle, a structure built by the Templars between 1214 and 1230, you can enjoy a fantastic view over the city and the course of the River Tagus. The medieval area around the castle is characterized by its narrow streets with unique names.

Another place to visit is the Garden of the sixteenth century Episcopal Palace. At the end of the eighteenth century, Bishop Vicente Ferrer, inspired by the baroque gardens, had the remarkable statues, stonework and box groves placed there. This garden has 3 levels, and 5 ponds with fountains, representing the 5 wounds of Christ. One of the ponds is composed of water tricks – the famous Italian Giochi. There is also a pond topped by the Moses waterfall, which highlights the beautiful water effect.

We would recommend a visit to the Cathedral, the construction of which dates back to the Middle Ages. Of note in this monument, which was dedicated to Saint Michael and which was the property of the Templars, is its gold leaf and also its paintings in its chancel and sacristy.

Monsanto, where every stone tells a story, belongs to the set of Historic Villages of Portugal. There, the houses capture our attention because, instead of the usual white, we see grey granite.

In 1165, Dom Afonso Henriques donated the lands of Monsanto to the Knights Templar. This was when the castle was built, which offers a beautiful view over the surroundings areas of this village, which was voted the "most Portuguese Village in Portugal". A replica of the prize, a silver rooster, is positioned at the top of the bell tower.

The dwellings built of stone are of particular note in this singular village. You can also visit the fifteenth century Mother Church, the Grotto and the Community Oven.

Monsanto view

Monsanto

Monsanto rooster

Idanha-a-Nova was separated from Idanha-a-Velha in 1206 and given to the Knights Templar. At that time, a defensive castle was built, which is now in ruins.

Of note in this municipality is the sixteenth century Mother Church, with a Renaissance portico and a beautiful dome. The Bell Tower, formerly used to warn the population of eminent dangers, has a weather vane to forecast the weather and show the direction of the wind.

Near Idanha, you can find the Marechal Carmona Dam which, joining the Ponsul and Torto rivers, is set in a quiet location, with varied vegetation, where in summer you can practise water sports.

Idanha-a-Nova view

Marshal Carmona reservoir

The mysteries of the Cities

Summer was the time for small discoveries. The blue sky released the wisps of grey clouds that bound our hands and marshalled our thoughts. The time of small discoveries could not be weighed or measured, or be given a fixed schedule. There was no signalling code to guide us. Our tongues tasted the heat of August. Earlier we had had the taste of eternal rain.

In Fátima we spoke of devotion. We analysed the gestures of the spirit and gave thanks for the shelters of the heart. We went to the Mira de Aire Caves to learn about the freshness of the stalactites and the system of limestone formations.

In Leiria, we went back to tales of Prince Charming, which had accompanied us in childhood, and in Óbidos we were the queens that cared for that chocolate-scented realm.

We wrote messages on the beach sands at Nazaré and respectfully accepted the force of its gigantic waves. We conversed with the setting sun in the bay at São Martinho do Porto, as the leaves of the trees were gently rocked by the wind.

In Tomar, we took hold of our reins and were fearful horsewomen, riding bravely through the historical sanctuary, through which wound a fast-flowing river.

We dressed up to enjoy the monuments of Santarém, drawn by the magic of the Gothic style, under an endless sun.

We traversed the greatness of the monastery of Batalha and along the History of Portugal. We were perplexed at the bravery of the baker of Aljubarrota. But ... it was only in Alcobaça that we felt in the presence of the majesty of the heart. The love of D. Pedro and D. Inês de Castro moved us. They told us that Inês had been killed by the executioners of D. Afonso IV, father of D. Pedro, who had ordered her fate for fear that he would lose his kingdom to Castile. They added that Pedro, on hearing of the sad fate of his beloved, wanted to make her queen, even after her death. The two tombs, facing each other awaiting the judgment day, were our greatest discovery of eternal love.

Susana Fonseca

ESTREMADURA AND RIBATEJO

City main view

Castle palace, Gothic arcade

Praça de Rodrigues Lobo

Leiria is located in the central part of Portugal and originally grew up around the mound of its castle. It is washed by the Lis and Lena rivers. The Castle in Leiria was ordered to be built by Dom Afonso Henriques, on a rocky hill, to protect the lands of Soure and Coimbra from attacks by the Moors. As such the settlement grew around the castle. In the 15th century, King Dom João I ordered a royal palace to be constructed inside the walls of the castle, with Gothic galleries to provide beautiful views over the city. You can also visit the Cathedral, built in the 16th century, which combines the Gothic with a Renaissance style, and the Convent of *Santo Agostinho* and the Sanctuary of *Nossa Senhora da Encarnação*. We would also recommend a visit to the Museum of Moving Image, to the Paper Windmill (Moinho de Papel) and to the Dona Julinha Agronomy Museum. At the Paper Windmill, you can experience first-hand traditional paper manufacturing and the milling of cereals. The Largo Cândido dos Reis is an attractive area due to the bars which animate the old part of the city. The Francisco Rodrigues Lobo square, named after the Portuguese poet, is home to a number of cafés and cultural events. Leiria has been remodelling the banks of the Lis river to make a number of attractive parks, public spaces, playgrounds and thematic bridges.

← Pages 78 / 79. Óbidos medieval town

D. Carlos I park

The city of **Caldas da Rainha** is known for its thermal spas and its ceramic heritage.

The origin of the spas is linked to the time when Queen Dona Leonor saw a group of people bathing in the hot muddy water. They explained to her that those waters soothed pains and healed wounds. The Queen suffered from an ulcer and after trying this, she was cured, and so ordered a spa town to be built which opened in 1485 and is the oldest in Europe.

The Dom Carlos I Park was designed to turn Caldas da Rainha into one of the premier spas in Europe. The pavilions in the park were designed to house the nurses and a hotel, but this did not in fact materialise. However, they continue to have an imposing presence. Inside the space we can find the José Malhoa Museum. This city has been an important centre for pottery centre, where Rafael Bordallo Pinheiro, a famous caricaturist, set up a Ceramics Technical College, the Factory of which produces Caldas porcelain, pieces of an exceptional quality. We would recommend a visit to the Ceramics Museum and to the Bordallo Pinheiro Porcelain Factory. Every day in the Praça da República, also known as the 'Praça da Fruta', there is an open air fruit and vegetable market.

Open air fruit and vegetable market

Ceramics museum

→ *Pages 82 / 83. (from up to the right)*
1- Batalha Monastery
2- Alcobaça Monastery (Inês de Castro)
3- Chapterhouse window, Cristo Convent, Tomar

Nossa Senhora de Fátima Basilica

Santíssima Trindade Basilica

Closely connected to the Christian Faith, **Fátima** is the place where it is believed that three young shepherds witnessed the apparitions of Our Lady, between 13 May and 13 October 1917. Nowadays the *Santuário de Nossa Senhora do Rosário*, located in Cova da Iria, is a place of pilgrimage, attracting the faithful from all over the world. The sanctuary consists of a set of buildings, as well as an extremely large open space. It is a meeting point for different cultures, united by the same faith. In the month of May it is usual to see thousands of pilgrims, from different parts of the country, walking on foot on the roads leading to Fátima, thus fulfilling their promises made to Our Lady. The place most visited in the courtyard of the Sanctuary is the *Capelinha das Aparições* which, along with a Holly Oak, marks one of the places where the apparitions occurred. The *Basílica de Nossa Senhora de Fátima*, built in the 20th century, has 15 altars, dedicated to the 15 mysteries of the Rosary, and panes of glass which represent the

Santíssima Trindade Basilica

Arrival of pilgrims

Candlelight procession

scenes of the apparitions of Our Lady. The tombs of the three young shepherds are located in this basilica. Since 2007 there has been the *Basílica da Santíssima Trindade* on the opposite side, in a circular format. Of note is its main entrance, made in bronze and around 8 m in height, dedicated to Christ.

There is a monument to the Sacred Heart of Jesus at the centre of the sanctuary, where there was once a well, the water of which has received many blessings.

Near the southern entrance of the sanctuary, you can see a piece of the Berlin Wall, which was placed there as it is believed that the fall of the Berlin Wall is linked to one of the secrets revealed by Our Lady to the three young shepherds.

Near the Sanctuary you can visit the Via Sacra, made up of 14 chapels marking the stations of Christ's Passion, as well as the houses of the three young shepherds, the Wax Museum and the Apparitions Museum.

Candlelight procession

Farewell to the Virgin Mary

Alcobaça Monastery

Alcobaça is bathed by the Coa and Baça rivers, names linked to the origin of the city's name.

The founding of the Monastery of Alcobaça dates from 1153, resulting from the interest of King Dom Afonso Henriques in populating these lands. Besides contributing to agricultural progress in the region, the cultural activity carried out by the monks of the Cistercian Order is also noteworthy. In the library they collected codices and copied important texts from the medieval period.

Alcobaça Monastery was the first monument in the country to be built entirely in the Gothic style and the second pantheon for the Portuguese monarchy.

The monastery church is a historical treasure, where you can visit the tombs of Dom Pedro and Dona Inês de Castro. The story of the love between Pedro and Inês will forever be linked to the monastery, since, according to legend, the couple will be reunited on Judgement Day. The tombs are some of the finest examples of medieval sculpture.

In the gallery to the east of the Cloister of Silence, there are still thirteenth century traces, such as the *Sala do Capítulo*, the *Dormitório*, the *Sala dos Monges* and the *Refeitório*.

Nazaré

Sítio Viewpoint

Nazaré is known for its beaches and natural heritage that can be admired from a number of viewpoints. A legend associates the name Nazareth to an image of the Virgin which came from Nazareth in Palestine. The image, which ended up in Portugal, was venerated by Dom Fuas Roupinho who, one foggy day, was hunting a deer and saw it disappear over a cliff. Startled, Dom Fuas appealed for help to the Virgin, and immediately his horse halted, saving the rider's life, who then had the *Ermida da Memória* built as a token of his thanks. The characteristic clothes of the city illustrate the traditional importance of the sea and fishing. It is told that women in Nazaré waited for their husbands and sons to return from their fishing trips sitting on the sand. They wore several skirts to cover and protect themselves from the cold. Nazaré is also known for its beaches and their excellent waves for surfing. The underwater canyon, known as the *Canhão* or the *Cana da Nazaré*, is the largest in Europe. The *Praia do Norte* has the biggest waves in Portugal. In 2011, *Norte do Canhão* entered the Guinness Book of Records thanks to the Hawaiian surfer Garrett McNamara, who surfed a wave of around 31 m, repeating the feat in 2013 with an even higher wave.

Cliffs

Main view over the bay

São Martinho do Porto beach

São Martinho do Porto is a beach resort that attracts tourists thanks to the beauty of its bay, with its fine sand and calm waters. Its beach forms a perfect clamshell and this endows it with singular properties for those who wish to swim in the water and use it for water sports. The bay forms the last vestige of the old gulf that once existed there. São Martinho do Porto grew in the form of an amphitheatre, from the chapel of Santo António to the dunes Salir. The bay of São Martinho do Porto used to be one of the main ports of the country. Nowadays, in addition to the marina, the beach is a centre for collecting underwater seaweed. Rare bird species such as the alpine swift, the blue rock thrush and the kestrel can be observed in the region. Given its proximity to the sea, temperatures are mild throughout most of the year.

Fishing port

Peniche – Praça Forte

Fort of St. John the Baptist in Berlengas

Peniche is known for its traditional link to fishing and its associated industries, and for its bobbin lace. The city is also known for its cuisine, particularly its fish stew. Since 2009, Peniche has been a part of the World Surfing Tour, with the *Supertubos* beach being the most famous. In addition to this sport, body board and diving are also widely practised. Of particular note amongst its vast patrimony is the Furninha Cave, the Church of Saint Peter and the 16th century Peniche fortress, which is located by the sea. It was used as a prison during the Salazar regime, and now houses the Municipal Museum. The Berlengas islands are visible from the coast and accessible by boat. *Berlenga Grande* is a nature reserve for nesting seabirds such as cormorants and seagulls.

Mira de Aire caves

The **Mira de Aire** caves near Fátima, in the district of Santarém, are the largest in Portugal. Their maximum depth is 110 metres. The caves were discovered in 1947, although they have only been open to the public in 1971. The visit starts with the presentation of a documentary about the formation of caves, followed by the *Sala Grande* (the Large Room - the first well), which owes its name to its grandeur, and the *Sala Vermelha* (the Red Room), named after the colour of the place. The second well is called *Cúpula Majestosa* (Majestic Cupola). After a steep descent to the Gallery, several limestone formations can be seen along the way, such as the *Alforreca* (Jellyfish) and the *Pequenos Lagos* (Small Lakes), among others. There are also small streams that flow into the *Large Lake*.

Batalha Monastery

The village of **Batalha** was founded by Dom João I, along with the Monastery of *Santa Maria da Vitória* to give thanks to the divine for help in the victory at the Battle (Batalha in Portuguese, hence the name of the city) of Aljubarrota, which was fought in 1385.

The monastery, work on which started in 1388, and lasted nearly two centuries, has three particularly important areas: the capela do *Fundador*, the *Capelas Imperfeitas* and the *Claustro Manuelino*. The first, which is the most magnificent tomb in Portugal, was conceived by Dom João I. It is laid out in the form of a gigantic octagon inscribed in a large square. A tombstone inscribed in Latin is located here, recalling the deeds of the king for posterity. All around the room are buried the so-called 'illustrious Generation'.

Dom Duarte planned to build a grand mausoleum, outside the church and connected to it by a monumental gateway. This was the nucleus known as the *Capelas Imperfeitas*. The project was never fully executed, which makes it an attractive mystery of the monument. The cloister and the smaller adjacent rooms would have been constructed at the behest of Dom Afonso V.

The monastery was considered a World Heritage Site by UNESCO in 2007 and is an example of late Portuguese Gothic architecture in the Manueline style.

The municipality of Batalha is also rich in natural heritage, notably the mountain landscape that includes the Natural Park of Serra de Aires and Candeeiros. Limestone is present in the caves, ravines and cliffs. Of note are the *Grutas da Moeda*, the *Gruta do Buraco Rito*, the *Pia da Ovelha* and the *Escarpa de Falha do Reguengo Fetal*.

Main view, Óbidos

Nocturnal view

Main view

Castle of Óbidos

The town of **Óbidos**, snuggling up to its wall, is considered charming due to its whitewashed houses. There is much to see and tell about this former queenly villa, which gives the town an aristocratic feel.

Óbidos was offered by Dom Dinis to Dona Isabel as a wedding gift. From that time onwards, the village was the dowry of several queens, and became known as Queen's House. Queen Isabel had the chapel of *São Vicente* (now the Igreja de São João) built, organized the Brotherhood of the *Divino Espírito Santo* and founded a convent of friars. Dona Leonor founded the *Misericórdias* and Dona Catarina had the aqueduct built. Throughout the twentieth century, Óbidos was included in national tourist itineraries. Its houses were purchased for vacation homes and the streets, which retain their ancient charm, filled with shops and craft. The castle was converted into a *pousada*, and was considered as one of the most fascinating historical places for tourists to visit in Portugal. Monuments to visit include the castle, the *Igreja de Santa Maria* with the impressive tomb of Dom João de Noronha and its large altarpieces with paintings by Josefa de Óbidos, the churches of *Misericórdia*, *São Miguel de Gaieiras* and o *Senhor da Pedra*; the *Porta da Vila* and the Chapels of *Santa Iria* and *Santa Ana*.

Óbidos is also known for its Chocolate Festival and also as the Christmas Village, two unmissable annual events.

You can also play on the golf course, go to the lagoon in Óbidos and the beaches, such as *Covões* and *d'El Rei*.

Rua Direita

Praça de Sá da Bandeira

View over river Tagus at "Portas do Sol" viewpoint

Almourol Castle, Vila Nova da Barquinha

There are many monuments to visit in **Santarém**, which is the capital of the Gothic style in Portugal. In the city centre, there is the church of *Nossa Senhora da Conceição do Colégio dos Jesuítas* also known as the *Igreja do Seminário* (Cathedral), which is a Baroque building with many windows. Upon entering the church of *Graça*, in the historical centre, you can find one of the most beautiful Portuguese Gothic monuments, housing the tomb of Pedro Álvares Cabral, the navigator who, in 1500, sailed into a Brazilian port. Only the *Torre das Cabaças* remains of the Castle in Santarém, known as the Clock Tower, and some sections of its walls, from where you can view the fortified enclosure of *Alcáçova*, the *Porta de Santiago* and the *Porta do Sol*. Alongside these there is a garden, where you can take in one of the most well-known views in in Portugal, that of the *lezíria*, the flatlands, and the Tagus.

There are other Gothic examples in the city, such as the *Fonte das Figueiras*, the *Igreja do Convento de Santa Clara*, and the convent of *São Francisco*.

Near Constância, there was a fortification on a rocky islet in the Tagus, where, in 1160, Gualdim Pais, Master of the Order of the Temple, ordered a castle to be built. You may wonder at its location since it situated on a high cliff and surrounded by deep water. However, the strategic location was chosen because the river was the main entrance into the country. This is one of the most beautiful and picturesque Portuguese castles, which has been a source of inspiration for stories and legends. To visit the interior of the castle, you need to cross the river in a boat.

Convent of Christ, cloisters

Convent of Christ

The castle complex and the **Convent of Christ**, founded by Gualdim Pais in 1160, was the military headquarters of the Templars until 1314. The octagonal *Charola* which forms part of the castle is a Romanesque sanctuary with an oriental influence. These buildings were classified as World Heritage by UNESCO, and they form the largest area of monuments in Portugal.

The Temple, which was handed over to the Order of Christ in 1357, has eight cloisters, lookouts and numerous chambers. After the dissolution of the orders, the temple has served as a court, barracks, jail, barn, finance office and even manor house for the Minister Costa Cabral.

The characteristic feature of the monument is its varying architectural styles. It is worth admiring the *Charola* (the original church of the Templars), the famous Chapter Window (in the Manueline style), with its marine motifs in honour of the Age of Discoveries and the Cloister of Dom João III.

Praça da República

Synagogue of Tomar

Nabão River

Tomar, Templar city, possesses a rich architectural heritage and is surrounded by a magical atmosphere that makes us think of a historical sanctuary.

The Knights Templar helped the first king of Portugal to conquer Santarém. As a reward for their deeds, the location now known as the Covent of Christ was ordered to be constructed. The *Igreja de Santa Maria do Olival* also belonged to the Order and served as a pantheon for its Masters. We can state that Tomar developed in two different areas: one being the convent and the other involved the contribution of the Jews along the bank of the Nabão River. The synagogue, which still can be visited, is the oldest in Portugal.

The city is rich in patrimony, of which can be highlighted the *Igreja de São João Baptista*, a church in the late Gothic style, and, in particular, its Tower.

The *Festa dos Tabuleiros* is held every 4 years in July. This is a must-see tradition, where women parade with trays laden with bread and flowers on their heads.

Enchanted Moon

My letter to you:

The changing moons bring about little change in the dark rustling of the road that leads to Sintra. Whomsoever dares to go thereupon senses that they go beyond a frontier and henceforth proceed in tacit agreement between Man and Nature. The first part obeys the laws of silence whereas the second, as an absolute monarch reigns ominously, using a voice comprised of the very sounds that shake the earth.

It was on a night with the moon dressed in white that I ventured into the Sintra hills in search of a gesture from your arms, arms that have now without explanation left me in a desert. Maybe it was an act of madness, impulse or something beyond my reckoning that simply dragged me down the road. I knew deep inside I would not find you there.

I stopped the car near a rock but the trees continued to pass me by. I stepped outside and sensed the smell of blood and resin. I saw a lady wearing lunar colours. She carried a jug under her arm and moaned like a wounded animal. I approached. She looked at me as to beg for help. Zaida was her name as she told me in a sweet voice that she knew I'd arrive.

She wished to take water to her noble lover who lay injured inside the cave, but he was unable to move. It was then that I noticed a spot of blood covering the left side on her chest.

I grabbed the jug and went into a cave lit by torches. I did the lady's asking. Her beloved drank greedily until sated. He offered me some water that was left and asked me to stay a little longer by his side. I sat next the injured man and my eyes grew heavy. I slumbered in a deep sleep, lulled by a gentle voice. I awoke with a flood of light from the sun's rays that tore through the walls of the cave and seeped into ground.

I stepped outside. My car was there. There was no evidence of the maid nor the man I had sated. I no longer sensed the smell of blood and felt strangely comforted. I found not your arm's gesture, but something impelled me to write you this letter.

Your's A.

This letter was found at Cova da Moura (Moor Cave), Sintra, on November 1, 2009.

Susana Fonseca

Palace Library

Mafra National Palace

40 kilometres from Lisbon, the **Palácio Nacional de Mafra** is located within the township of Mafra. Also called the Mafra Royal Convent, it was built by King João V to fulfill a vow of succession. This is the most important of Portuguese Baroque monuments. It encompasses a basilica, a royal palace and a convent of the Order of St. Francis.

German goldsmith Johan Friedrich Ludwig, trained as an architect in Italy, was in charge of this work which began in 1717 and finished in 1770, mobilizing tens of thousands of workers and teachers of the various arts, a work considered as the seed for the first school of sculpture in the country.

On the king's 41st birthday, 22 October 1730, was the solemn inauguration of the basilica, festivities that lasted a week. The building houses one of the most significant Portuguese libraries.

It has approximately 40,000 volumes and numerous works of art commissioned by the monarch. The library's books deal with topics such as Civil and Ecclesiastical Law, Medicine and Physics. Some say that bats residing therein aid in the conservation, preventing the destruction of works by moths.

There are many legends regarding the convent, the most popular of these relating to the existence of huge rats in the palace's underground.

The Mafra National Palace was classified as a National Monument in 1910 and was finalist upon the election of the Seven Wonders of Portugal, in 2007.

← Págs. 98 / 99. Largo do Chiado

Queluz National Palace

The **Palácio Nacional de Queluz** is one of the finest Portuguese palaces and has extraordinary gardens. It was built by King Pedro III in 1747 under the direction of architect Mateus Vicente de Oliveira. It was the favourite summer residence for the royal family at the end of the 17th century.

The palace is often compared to Versailles although it has many Portuguese characteristics and its scale is so different. It is surrounded by fifteen hectares of gardens which in turn are embellished by numerous lakes, plus stone and lead sculptures from Italy and England that provide visitors with a journey through Ancient Classical Mythology. The upper gardens were designed by French architect-sculptor Jean-Baptiste Robillion and show a strong French influence.

Several thematic locations are highlighted as follows: the "Jardim Novo" or Malta Garden, Pênsil or Grand Garden, the Great Cascade, Lakes of Neptune, Amphitrite of Medals, and the Tile channels.

It has served for leisure and entertainment to the royal family whom had attended there shows of fire works, bullfights, and games of chivalry known as *Cavalhadas*. Presently in the summer these palatial gardens remain

Throne Hall

a privileged space for the conducting of outdoor events such as musical performance, and dance among others. The Portuguese School of Equestrian Art performs equestrian activities at its New Riding Arena.

Monserrate palace

The **Palácio de Monserrate** is part of Monserrate Park. This palace was designed in mid-nineteenth century by English architect James T. Hair Knowles to serve as a summer residence for the Cook family. The architect had to adapt the project to existing ruins of a neo-Gothic mansion. The building that was erected is original and eclectic. The edifice's domes, red doors and Gothic inspired windows stand out. The interiors are lush, full of eastern influences, especially in the gallery - the "Music Hall" where classical and Indian themes are combined. The superb gardens where one can find over 3000 exotic species form a magnificent whole, deserving full attention upon visit as had done poet - Lord Byron, in 1809.

Monserrate palace

Pena Palace

Pena Palace

Adamastor

Palácio da Pena was built by D. Fernando Coburg-Gotha in the nineteenth century. Influenced by the eclectic and Romantic trends of the time, D. Fernando II, married to D. Maria II, chose a revivalist palace with the artistic traditions from antiquity to the Renaissance. In addition we find the influence of Eastern art, domes, minarets and Mudejars, and the decorative Manueline style. To oversee the work the Baron of Eschwege was summoned, he in turn was inspired by the palaces of Bavaria. At 500 metres of altitude the Palácio da Pena comprises the most complete and admirable example of Portuguese Romantic architecture, warming hearts of fantasy as if it were the sun itself. From the Palace the visitor can see Pena Park, a blanket of trees that entices one to walk through idyllic paths of numerous gardens among other pleasures worthy of royalty.

Quinta da Regaleira

The Castelo dos Mouros

The **Quinta da Regaleira** (Regaleira Estate) is located in the historic centre of Sintra, a town classified as World Heritage by UNESCO. Built in the early twentieth century the Regaleira Estate is the result of the achieving of estate owner António Augusto Carvalho Monteiro's vision. To do so he commissioned the Italian architect and designer Luigi Manini the work. Out of the imaginings of these two figures came a summation of varied artistic trends, with particular emphasis on the Gothic, Renaissance and Manueline, while not forgetting to reminisce in the nation's historic mythical and esoteric tradition.

Regaleira has within it a palace, chapel, stables and various underground buildings. It is a surprising and unforgettable monument where one can behold a world full of symbols.

The **Moorish Castle** (*Castelo dos Mouros*), also called the Castle of Sintra, was founded by the Muslims in the 9th century. It was constructed on a rocky mass on the ridges of the Serra de Sintra. High on its walls, you can make out the surrounding villages, Sintra and Pena Palace.

This castle was never the stage of a battle, for its function would have been to monitor the Lisbon region. With the continuous advancement of the *Reconquista* to the South, the Moorish Castle lost its strategic importance. In the 19th century, King Fernando had to restore the old fortress, which means that nowadays there is little to be seen of the original castle, except the base of the towers and the walls.

Sintra National Palace

Sintra National Palace

Palácio Nacional de Sintra is located in the historic centre of Sintra. It was built upon a former royal Muslim residence, having become the property of Portuguese kings for over eight centuries. The present building underwent successive modifications. King Manuel I ordered the construction of the east wing, well known for its exquisite window ornamentation. It was also this monarch's initiative to build the tower for the Blazon Hall of Arms, and the redecorating of the palace with coats of existing tile giving it its singular Mudejar character that it still preserves today. During his reign there were several evening feasts in the presence of the king himself with Moor musicians and artistic figures from court - Gil Vicente for instance.

The palace has been inhabited for long periods time, either to provide support for hunting, or as a refuge from Lisbon during the summer months. The interior has collections of furniture, paintings, ceramics and textiles dating from the 16th to the 19th century.

There are several halls endowed with specific features that leave visitors enchanted. The kitchens are especially known for their conical chimneys of monumental proportions. Its 'profile' has long been a distinguishing characteristic marking Sintra's landscape; a town along with its collection of monuments classified in 1995 by UNESCO as being World Heritage Site.

São Jorge Castle

The **Castelo de São Jorge** is a National Monument of historical, archaeological and architectonical importance. The castle exists since the 11th century, a time when Lisbon was a major Muslim seaport. In 1147, the first king of Portugal Afonso Henriques, conquered the castle and the city from the Moors. From the 12th century to the beginning of the 16th century, the castle was a Royal Palace which received illustrious men, such as Gil Vicente , a great play-writer who presented at this place his first play. Life in the Court turned the castle into a privileged place, where King Manuel welcomed Vasco da Gama on his return from India. The transfer of the royal residence to downtown and the earthquake of 1755 marked the decay of the castle which was subject to restoration works in the 20th century that conferred it the present importance and recovered its priceless historical value. Today, on the eastern part of the castle named Praça Nova lies the Archaeological Centre, where remains from most ancient occupation of the area can be found and which date from the 7th century BC. The Museum at the Castle shows a collection of objects which allow the visitor to discover multiple cultures and experiences which helped to build the Lisbon we know today. The Periscope – the Tower of Ulysses – is situated in one of the castle´s towers and allows a panoramic view of the city of 360 – degree, in real time. Standing on the highest hill of the historical centre, the castle offers its visitors one of the nicest views over the city and the Tagus estuary.

← *Pages 106 / 107. (from up to the right) 01- View from Graça Belvedere 02- Streetcar at Praça do Comércio | 03- Fado in the streetcar*

Originally called Igreja de St. Maria Maior (The Patriarchal Cathedral of St. Mary Major), in 1150 King Afonso I of Portugal ordered the constructing of the **Sé de Lisboa** (Lisbon Cathedral), an edifice that clearly takes its inspiration from the Old Cathedral of Coimbra's Romanesque style architecture. Nevertheless in the present day it shows a mix of styles due to successive modifications and restorations over the centuries. The cathedral underwent transformation such as the construction of the Bartolomeu Joanes Chapel and the King Dinis cloister, both serving to exemplify Gothic, Portuguese cloisters; and the new main chapel plus an ambulatory built by King Afonso IV was added. The Franciscan chapel contains the sink where St. António was baptized in 1195 and is decorated with tiles showing the saint preaching to fish. In the adjacent chapel, there is a Baroque nativity scene made from cork, wood and terracotta by Machado de Castro.

The façade and the magnificent rose window in stained glass maintain their Romanesque appearance. The interior is dark for the most part, it is simple and austere. The Gothic cloister contains dainty double arches with beautiful carved capitals. One of the chapels has a thirteenth century iron wrought gate. Excavation within the cloisters has left important Roman remains out in the open for all to see.

Lisbon Cathedral

View over the cathedral

Jerónimos Monastery

Mosteiro dos Jerónimos (Hieronymites Monastery), built in the late Gothic style of architecture known as "Manueline", is located in Belém. It replaced a small chapel founded by Prince Henry (Infante D. Henrique) where monks from the Order of Christ gave assistance to sailors. King Manuel built it so as to make a pantheon for the members of his dynasty, dedicating the edifice to the Virgin of Belém (Virgin of "Bethlehem"). Construction began by 1501 and was finished a century later. The king channeled large sums, from revenues of trade with Africa and the East, for the endeavour. Much of said money came from profits from the spice trade, the so called 'Pepper Route'. To occupy the monastery king Manuel chose monks belonging to the Order of St. Jerónimo. Their main function was to pray for the the King's soul and salvation, as well as providing spiritual support for sailors and navigators that would set forth from the "Restelo Beach" with hopes of discovering more of the New World. Connected thus at the earliest stages in its life to the epic "Age of Discoveries", the monastery has practically always been associated to and held as being a symbol of the nation. During the nineteenth century it underwent various expansions and renovations giving it its present day look. Today the monument lets the viewer behold a blend of different styles: Renaissance, late Gothic and Manueline. Notable is the cloister and the South Gate of complex geometric design facing the River Tagus. The decorative elements are full of symbols of Nautical art along with sculptures of exotic plants and animals.The monument is considered World Heritage by UNESCO and on July 7th - 2007 it was elected as being one of the country's 'Seven Wonders'. Within it are tombs of some monarchs: Manuel I of Portugal, his wife Queen Maria, João III of Portugal, his wife Queen Catarina, D. Sebastião, D. Henrique, as well as the tombs of Vasco da Gama, Luís Vaz de Camões, Alexandre Herculano, and Fernando Pessoa.

Jerónimos Monastery

Jerónimos Monastery, cloisters

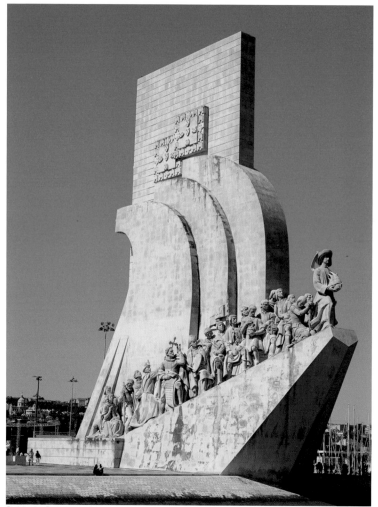

Padrão dos Descobrimentos

Henry, the navigator

The **Padrão dos Descobrimentos** (monument to the Age of Discoveries) was inaugurated in Belém in 1960 and was a strong presence in the memorial celebrations for the 500 years since the death of Prince D. Henrique the Navigator, the great patron of early European exploration. The sculpted composition consists of 33 figures connected to the Age of Discoveries, with Prince Henrique at the bow.

Access to the monument is decorated with a wind rose and world map, where one can see all the routes of Portuguese Exploration. This decoration executed in marble was offered by the Republic of South Africa. People can visit the look-out at the top, the auditorium and two showrooms.

The panorama from the viewpoint is impressive, with all the beauty of the River Tagus to one side and the majestic Hieronymites Monastery to the other.

Tower of Belém

The **Torre de Belém** (Tower of Belém) protrudes from the waters of the Tagus and is located where Belém beach used to be.

Built in the 16th Century it was part of the the Tagus estuary defensive plan that would protect the city (then the capital of a vast maritime empire) from piracy attacks or possible attacks of enemy nations.

With the development of other means for attack and defense, this structure lost its original function and was thenceforth used over the centuries for other purposes such as customs registration, telegraphy and as being a lighthouse. Its bunkers were used as dungeons for holding political prisoners.

This fortification has a bulwark and a square tower. Its shape is reminiscent of the towers within medieval castles. Much of its beauty comes from exterior details in Manueline style decor. One can see carved in stone: rope and tied knots, animal and plant motifs, religious statuary, open galleries, guard towers and battlements in the Moorish - shield-shaped – style. Quite unusual in other constructions of the gender this is a wonderful building. It blends all the requirements of military engineering with aesthetic care.

It is one of Lisbon's most expressive and symbolic monuments, classified by UNESCO as World Cultural Heritage.

Rua Augusta

Rua Augusta is one of the most famous downtown Lisbon streets. It starts at the magnificent triumphal arch and connects the city's Commerce Square to Rossio. It is a street full of commercial activity, with a variety of shops and stores on both sides. Street artists, artisans and vendors are also part of this street's life, making it one of the city's most lively routes during the day.

Praça do Comércio

Praça do Comércio is in downtown Lisbon and located next to the River Tagus in the area which used to be part of the palace of Portuguese kings for nearly two centuries. It is one of the largest squares in Europe. In 1511 King Manuel I moved his residence from the Castle of São Jorge to this location but the *Ribeira* (Riverside) Palace was totally razed following the 1755 earthquake. In the reconstructing of downtown Lisbon the plaza became the core element the Marquis of Pombal's plan. Buildings lined with arcades surrounding the square are now home to some departments of various ministries of the Portuguese government, and also the famous *Café Martinho da Arcada* - the oldest in Lisbon and one

of Fernando Pessoa's favourites. The yellow tones on these buildings within this wide area facing the river offer visitors a journey somewhere between dreams and reality. In the centre of the square one finds the statue of King José I, erected in 1775 by Machado de Castro. On the north side of the square is the Triumphal Arch of *Rua Augusta*. It is the entrance to the downtown district. This refurbished plaza also became part of Portugal's history through the 1908 regicide of Dom Carlos, and the revolt of the armed forces that overthrew the government in 1974. This square later had also served as a car park but today this vast space is used for cultural events and shows.

Panoramic view from Elevador de Santa Justa viewpoint

Elevador de Santa Justa

The Unusual neogothic style monument also known as the "Carmo Lift", the **Elevador de Santa Justa** (Santa Justa lift), was built in the historic centre of Lisbon. The elevator links the streets Rua do Ouro and Rua do Carmo to the city's historic Carmo Square.

The structure was designed and built in iron with lacy embellishments by engineer Raoul Mesnier du Ponsard at the turn of the century (19th to 20th). In its early years the lift was steam-driven, only later did it come to be electrically powered. It was considered at the time as being a bold piece of work for various reasons: the overcoming of the steep slope, materials used, and the viaducts built that bridge the different levels thus permitting access to the upper part of the city's hill known as "Carmo". Passengers can climb or go down one of the lift's elaborate booths. The views from the top floor are magnificent and allow one to see the Rossio, Lisbon's downtown, the Castle of São Jorge, the River Tagus, and the ruins of the Carmo Convent Church.

← Pages 116 / 117.
(left) Streetcar at Alfama
(right) Elevador da Bica

Fountain, Praça do Rossio

Detail from a Portuguese pavement

Rossio Railway station

Praça D. Pedro IV, better known as **Rossio**, is one of the busiest and most beautiful squares in Lisbon where thousands of people commute every day, most of them being on their way to a variety of destinations. It was named after King Pedro IV due to there being in its centre an imposing statue of this Portuguese king (and first emperor of independent Brazil). At the base of the statue there are four female figures each representing Justice, Wisdom, Strength and Moderation; all being qualities attributed to the king. The Pombaline style buildings surrounding the Square are filled with souvenir shops, jewellery stores and cafés. Noteworthy among these cafés is the Café Nicola - a living tribute to the Portuguese poet, Bocage.

By the middle of the 19th century the square was paved in wavy patterns of black and white cobblestones. At the north side lies the beautiful National Theatre D. Maria II. Another magnificent edifice impossible to go unnoticed is the Rossio train station with its dazzling neo-Manueline style façade.

Fado house "Dragão de Alfama"

Fado house "Bacalhau de Molho"

Pátio de Chanceller

Fado became popular back in 19th century Lisbon during moments of leisure and conviviality. It spontaneously became manifest in the streets, alleys, gardens, in the run of bulls, taverns and in cafés of chambermaids. Initially Fado was linked to a social context characterized by crime and transgression. Many sources evoke the involvement of aristocrats and Fado singing harlots. This is pictured and mentioned in many poems, sung in films, the theater, visual arts, and literature.

Revista type theatre included the singing of this music and thus making it reach a wider audience through renowned artists and Fado singers. The emergence of Fado companies allowed the promotion of professional performances and international tours. Gradually this music would be heard in Fado houses, places which would mainly be rooted within the city's historic neighbourhoods.

The **Fado Museum**, opened in 1998, is a museum devoted to the world of fado and guitar. It is located in the *Alfama* district. It is a cultural space with a permanent exhibition, a Documentation Centre, and a store among other spaces. It is entirely devoted to the world of Lisbon's urban musical genre. It celebrates the exceptional value of Fado as an identifying symbol of Lisbon.

Fado museum

Amália Rodrigues

Lisbon popular marches - Alfama unit

Party at Bairro Alto

Grilling sardines

Selling basils

The St. António festivity is one of the best known and liveliest fests in Portugal.

The "popular marches" that take place at Avenida da Liberdade began in 1932. It is a great night attraction. The avenue is thus filled with light, colour, dance, the rhythmic pace of the music (marches), and the joy of those participating in a unique festival in their town. Parading by civil parish, one can see the the result of the year's work. In hopes of being recognized by the jury and thus winning the contest each parish group comes forth with the lyrics, music and choreography for songs; dressing themselves accordingly based on each year's theme. Every year the parochial rivalries spur each neighbourhood to show its best. The jury ultimately casts its vote, and not always in agreement with the opinions of viewers and participants. With many public figures and municipal politicians, participating among them - the mayor. This event is broadcast by national television. Each neighbourhood invites a man and woman, usually acclaimed figures from the entertainment business to be their 'godfathers' for the night.

Streetcar at Alfama

Alfama panoramic view

Of Lisbon's various quarters, **Alfama** is one of the most typical. Everything here seems to come from the timeless power of memory: narrow streets, steep stairways, tile façades on houses, clothes lines, vases full of flowers, cats that creep in and onto balconies, neighbours who talk about the weather and the state of things, children running, and passing visitors who take pictures of glimpsing moments so as to later recollect. Views from Alfama of the cityscape and River Tagus inspire and are a haven for thought. Viewpoints include: Portas do Sol, Santa Luzia, the São Jorge Castle, the Church of São Vicente de Fora, and the National Pantheon among other places. Amidst houses and courtyards one finds traces of Roman and Arabic occupation. The Lisbon Cathedral shows the passage of time and reflects a mix of architectural styles. During the Summer fests that celebrate the Saints, especially "Santo António", the streets teem with people, sardines and basil. Every morning Alfama awakens to the sound of streetcars and every night slumbers to the sound of guitars playing in Fado houses.

Rossio dos Olivais

Water volcano

Oceanário

Oceanário

The **Parque das Nações** is currently the name of the place where the notorious World Expo 1998 was held. This event led to the revitalization of the area east of the city turning it into a prestigious cultural centre dominated by modern architecture with housing and business.

If we access this area through the Oriente Station, designed by Spanish architect Santiago Calatrava, we are faced with the towering iron arches, and the impressive columns and arches of reinforced concrete. Walking through innovative Shopping centre "Vasco da Gama" we see the Atlantic Pavilion (Altice Arena) and the Pavilion of Portugal. The later is by Portuguese architect Álvaro Siza Vieira. It bares the impressive concrete visor that resembles a sheet of paper placed on two bricks. One of the most visited places and attractions of this park is the Oceanarium - one of the largest aquariums in the world. It recreates for visitors four oceans, where there are sharks, barracudas, stingrays and mantarays. We can also ride the chairlift and admire the Vasco da Gama Tower, the tallest building in the city at 142 metres.

Parque das Nações

Atlantic Pavilion (Altice Arena)

Oriente train station

Cascais Marina

Bay of Cascais

The **Cascais Marina** is home to numerous luxury yachts. It also has shops, diverse spots of leisure and is an international stage for sporting events. It has inclusively received a World Cup Sailing Championship. The **Bay of Cascais** has lent its name to a title of a well known song and is considered one of the most beautiful spots within the city. Both areas are great places to stroll and relax.

Casa das Histórias

Museum

The **Casa das Histórias de Paula Rego** is a museum that displays part of the body of work by the artist and that of her husband, Victor Willing (artist and art critic) who had died in 1988. The Museum's design is by Souto de Moura, an architect chosen for the task by the artist herself. The building has 750 m² for exhibit areas, a shop, a café and an auditorium with 200 seats.

In accordance to the artist's own wishes the museum should be a space for "fun, be unpretentious, alive, full of joy and much mischief".

The collection is on a rotating basis. Paula Rego was born in Portugal but has lived and worked in London for a long time. Beyond a doubt she is one of the most prestigious national artists.

Fishing port

Walls of Setúbal, Porta de São Sebastião

Setúbal is located on the site of a former Roman town with activities related to fish salting and the production of ceramics. During the 15th century, the city became a popular resort for the aristocracy.

In the historical centre, between the two lines of walls, stand a group of monuments such as the Church and the Convent of Jesus, a building in the Manueline style, with a stately interior with arches, windows and columns made of breccia, a characteristic stone of the *Serra da Arrábida*. Opposite the church is the *Cruzeiro de Setúbal*, also made of breccia.

Lower down, you will find the *Praça de Bocage*, which owes its name to the famous Setúbal poet, whose statue stands in the centre of the square. This is a great space to socialise and take a little break. In this square, visit the *Igreja de São Julião*, an imposing church with Manueline gates, with its tiles inside telling the story of Saint Julian.

Continue your walk to the São Sebastião viewpoint, where you can enjoy the fantastic views that this pleasant site affords. From the *Serra da Arrábida* to *Tróia*, everything is reflected in the sheen of the Sado River.

Panoramic view from the Castle of Palmela

Palmela was conquered by Dom Afonso Henriques in 1147, and was previously occupied by the Celts, Romans and Arabs because of its strategic position. This village, rich in history and heritage, will take you on a journey back in time. If you climb up to the castle, you can make out the Sado estuary, the *Serra da Arrábida* and the plains of the River Tagus from the top of the Keep.

Within the walls is the 15th century Church of Santiago, built in a late Gothic style. Under a tomb lodged in a wall, you can see what is thought to be the tomb of King Jorge, the last Master of the Order of Santiago. You can also visit the Clock Tower. We would also recommend a trip to the Church of Santa Maria, built in the 12th century. Despite being in ruins due to the 1755 earthquake, this church has a Renaissance funerary chapel and some remains of its 17th century tiles.

Finally, if you wish to stay overnight here, be sure to stop by the old Convent of the Order of Santiago, built in the 15th century and now transformed into a luxurious *pousada*.

Castle of Palmela

Palmela main view

Panoramic view over Sesimbra

Cliffs at Parque Natural da Arrábida

Lighthouse of Cabo Espichel

Sesimbra is a traditional fishing town where you can visit its castle, standing on top of the hill, the last overlooking the sea that still retains its medieval layout.

In the city centre there is the Sea Museum and the Museum of Archaeology. By the coast you will find the Fortress of Santiago, built in the seventeenth century. Overlooking the sandy beaches of Sesimbra, this fort offers a beautiful view.

Cape Espichel is a location remarkable for the intensity of the surrounding sea, the passage of migratory birds, its geological richness and the diversity of its flora. The Chapel was built in the fifteenth century and there is a set of tiles inside representing the apparition of Our Lady of the Cape in 1410 and the construction of the Sanctuary. The Lighthouse, with its hexagonal tower, started operations in 1790 and is illuminated by olive oil. There is a legend associated with this site, which tells of an inhabitant of Alcabideche who in 1410 saw a very bright star over the Cape. It is said that the light was an apparition of Our Lady of the Cape, there to calm the storm and illuminate the ocean. Popular wisdom has it that the light appeared in exactly the same spot where nowadays the light from the lighthouse is focused.

Parque Natural da Arrábida

If there are places in Portugal we can fall in love with, then the **Serra da Arrábida** is undoubtedly one of them. The surrounding landscape is the result of a combination of mountains and sea coast. Its limestone and millennial formation make it a unique example of primitive Mediterranean vegetation. In 1976, the Serra da Arrábida was declared a Natural Park. Make sure to visit the *Convento da Arrábida*, founded in 1542 by Franciscan friars. They took a vow of poverty and spent two years living in cells carved out of the rocks. On the coast, you will find some of the best beaches in the region, such as *Portinho da Arrábida* or *Praia Galapos*, where the blue transparent water and the beauty of the landscape will make you think that you have arrived in paradise. There is a path you can take as suggested by the Institute of Nature Conservation, which will take you to several points of interest, such as the *Miradouro das Antenas* with its great view over the beaches, the *Miradouro da Santa*, which offers magnificent panoramic landscapes over the protected area, as well as many other places that will surprise you.

The Seamstress

At the time when the plains belonged to me, I was twelve. I do not know how many years have passed, but I know that today, looking out of the attic window down on the white houses, I see the characters belonging to stories I imagine while I sew. People pass, sheltered from the sun, and seem to belong to a different world to that of mine.

Sometimes I cannot separate myself from my sewing machine, as if it were an extension of my body. My hands work nonstop. I sew in the morning and in the afternoon heat with no end in sight. Sometimes I let the work continue into the moonlit nights.

Some people get scared when they hear me working. Perhaps because of the deafening noise of the pedals, the precise sound of the cutting of the fabric or the echo that the scissors produce when I place them on the wood. I do not stop working within the whitewashed houses. I want to line the walls with my fabrics and wander from house to house until someone stops me. Each machine becomes a house and I am unable to stop.

At the time when I was not an extension of a sewing machine, I used to walk through the plains down to the rivers. I picked green herbs and vine leaves. My mother made bread dumplings with the former and baked beans with the latter. Those meals filled me day after day. Sometimes I walked with my father through the landscapes interspersed with oaks and olive trees. I could smell wheat and barley. We climbed up to the castle and he spoke to me of the Arab influences on Nature and people. My days belonged to me.

Until the time came when the plains slipped from my feet, and so, without realizing how or why, I found myself alone.

Now I wander through the houses sewing and shaping a world of plains with the fabrics. People do not see me and I do not understand why I make so much noise. If anyone would be so kind as to offer me company, perhaps I could stop and rest.

Susana Fonseca

ALENTEJO

Castle of Estremoz

Castle of Evoramonte

Estremoz main view

Evoramonte

Known for its white marble, the city of **Estremoz** is located at the intersection of two major roads (Faro-Guarda and Lisbon-Madrid). When looking at the city from afar, we can see the Keep, surrounded by the walls and whitewashed houses.

The Castle of Estremoz, from where you can observe the main features of the Serra da Estrela, is in Largo Dom Dinis, which houses a number of monuments, such as the aforementioned Keep, an interesting example of Gothic architecture. We would recommend a visit to the *Capela Rainha Santa Isabel* which in the 18th century was enlarged and enriched with paintings and tiles depicting the life and miracles of Isabel of Aragon.

The Marquês de Pombal square has stalls featuring local produce, shops and monuments, including the Museum of Sacred Art. Another monument is the Town Hall, with its various tile panels depicting the costumes and habits of different social classes at the time of Dom João V.

Near Estremoz is Evoramonte, a parish located in the Serra d'Ossa. At the top of the hill there is a castle built using masonry and ashlar granite in a rectangular shape, combining both Gothic and Renaissance styles.

Ducal Palace

Sanctuary of Nossa Senhora da Conceição

Typical houses

Vila Viçosa, known for the abundance of its pink marble, features numerous monuments of great interest, such as the 13th century castle and the Pelourinho (pillory), standing 8 metres high and designed in a Gothic-Manueline style. Within the walls you can discover the shrine dedicated to *Nossa Senhora da Conceição*, considered Queen and Patron Saint of Portugal.

The Ducal Palace is located in the centre of the town, which for centuries was the seat of the House of Braganza, an important royal dynasty. Construction of the building began in 1501, and it has a classical façade 110 metres long. In the palace you can find paintings, sculpture, furniture, tapestry, ceramics and jewellery collections. During the visit, you can also enjoy the decor, which has remained unchanged, including the 17th century tiles, the beautiful paintings on the ceilings and the marble fireplaces. We would also highlight the remarkable and impressive kitchen full of copper utensils, as well as the Library and a section of the Coach Museum.

Arraiolos carpet embroiderer

Castle of Arraiolos

Convent of Lóios

Arraiolos, a village in the Alentejo, has been known for its beautiful carpets and hand embroidery for generations. In the village centre there is a pleasant square where you can enjoy the local shops, have some refreshments and even, if you are lucky, watching an Arraiolos carpet being made.

Slightly out of the centre, two monuments worth visiting are the Arraiolos Castle and the Lóios Convent. The castle stands at the top of the hill. It is also known as the *Paço dos Alcaides* and was built in 1305 to defend the region from attacks by the Moors. It is one of the few in the world to have a circular configuration.

The Convent of Lóios, dedicated to Our Lady of the Assumption and built in 1575, belonged to the Order of Saint Eloi. Nowadays the building has been transformed into a *pousada* and the church is open to the public. It is worth visiting it for its tiles and its standard religious motifs. Of note as well is its quadrangular bell tower.

Town main view

Elvas

Amoreira Aqueduct

Forte de Santa Luzia

Located in a border area, **Elvas** was conquered from the Arabs by Dom Sancho II in 1228. Its military history has left its mark, and the centre of Elvas still "embraces" its seventeenth-century ramparts, the highest point of which is the castle. The fort of Santa Luzia and that of Graça, alongside the wall, form a triple defence line.

In the centre of town there is the Praça da República, which contains the Cathedral and several mansion houses. The well-conserved *Pelourinho* (Pillory) rests on a pedestal containing five steps. The quadrangular *Torre Fernandina* was used as the jail from the 15th century onwards.

The *Aqueduto da Amoreira*, consisting of 843 arches, was built to solve the city's water supply. The *Forte da Graça*, which was founded by the great-grandfather of Vasco da Gama, contained around 80 cannon, with wells and underground galleries encircling the fortification. The *Forte de Santa Luzia* houses the Military Museum, which has an exhibition of objects used by the garrisons, such as weapons and military equipment. Visitors can also enjoy discovering one of the subterranean galleries that run through part of the fort and which served as a refuge and storage area in the event of an invasion.

Campo Maior

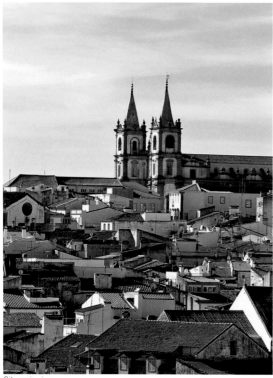

Portalegre is known as the city of the seven convents, of which only five remain: that of São Francisco (which houses religious art), Santo Agostinho, Santa Clara (the Municipal Library), Santo António and São Bernardo. We would recommend a visit to the Cathedral, particularly to see the beautiful hand-painted altars enriched with gold-leaf, and the Mannerist paintings. In the sacristy, you can appreciate the coat of arms of Portugal, the huge chandeliers and the tiles.

The castle, which dates back to 1290, was built to protect this border area. Although it is not possible to walk along the walls, there is an inner structure which allows you to view it from different heights.

The *Palácio Amarelo* (Yellow Palace), set in the medieval fabric, is a landmark of the Baroque. Although the building is not open to the public, it is worth taking in its façade, with its 11 windows protected by iron railings, suggesting a house belonging to the gentry. You can visit the Guy Fino Portalegre Museum of Tapestry, dedicated to the "Portalegre Stich" and honouring this artistic heritage. There is a giant sycamore, 173 years old, in the centre of the city, which has been classified as a "tree of public interest".

City main view

Marvão and its wall

Castle of Marvão

Marvão

Marvão, situated on a plateau of the Serra de São Mamede, seems to belong to another era, taking visitors on a journey into the past.

Its history dates back to the Muslim era, when Ibn Marwan, an important authority in the Muslim Empire, conquered the region and rebuilt the fortifications in the mountains. Marwan gave his name to the settlement, which led to the current place name.

The architecture of the place and the stunning scenery make it a very memorable location. Prepare yourself to stroll through characteristic streets, such as *Rua do Espírito Santo, do Castelo* and *das Portas de Vila*. We would recommend a visit to the Old Town Hall, in the Manueline style, which houses the old prison, and also a visit to the Clock Tower and the old courthouse. The parts of the castle are interconnected, and it has a huge cistern that houses the Military Museum Centre, where historical information is available on the town and the castle and which also has an exhibition of pieces of armour. A characteristic of the town is the white houses nestling inside the city wall, which will surely provide you with a fine memory of the city.

View over Alqueva

Castle of Monsaraz

Alqueva became better known due to the construction of its dam, which is the seventh largest in Portugal. Its lake, considered to be the largest artificial lake in Europe, and the superb scenery offer visitors a range of leisure activities, such as boating, staying on a boat and other water sport activities. You can also "put your best foot forward" and explore tracks on foot, bicycle, horseback or using a 4x4 vehicle.

You can visit several villages, such as *Amieira*, *Pedrógão* and *Aldeia da Luz*, where you can have the opportunity to see typical houses and enjoy a number of regional dishes. **Monsaraz** stands out in this regard. This walled villa offers a spectacular view, including over Alqueva. The castle is somewhat peculiar, being of the few with an arena which takes us back to the time of gladiators and their mortal combats.

Monsaraz

Castle of Monsaraz

Monsaraz

Castle of Monsaraz

Pillory

Church of Santa Maria

Vila Romana de Pisões

Convent of São Francisco

Beja was the birthplace of many Renaissance educators and humanists. It is believed to have been founded in 400 BC by the Celtic people and conquered by the Christians in 1162. Formerly named *Pax Julia*, the town thrived during the presence of the Romans as can be seen by the pieces on exhibition at the Rainha Dona Leonor Museum.

One of its historical landmarks is the castle, and its keep is one of the finest examples of military architecture in Portugal. Next to the castle, there is a Roman arch,

located at the intersection of two main roads that bears witness to the ideal model Roman city. Right next to this you can visit Beja Cathedral richly decorated in gold leaf. The inside contains a beautiful image of the Sacred Heart of Jesus and its 17th century altars are complemented by blue and white tiles.

In the main square of the city, you can visit the 16th century *Igreja da Misericórdia*, a church in the Renaissance style inspired by the famous Loggia in Florence. Next to the Church we can find the

Castle of Beja

Pelourinho (Pillory), on which we can see the emblems of King Dom Manuel, the armillary sphere and the iron cross of Christ. The Museum annex at Rua do Sembrano has an exhibition consisting of a number of archaeological structures. These vestiges from Pre-History to the Contemporary Era illustrate the story of those who lived, worked, suffered and loved here. The *Villa Romana Pisões* is near to Beja and was accidentally discovered in 1967. It is a dwelling from the Roman period which was occupied between the first and fourth centuries B.C. It would have contained more than 40 richly decorated rooms, where the cult of the body must have been its main focus, since a number of rooms were dedicated to this, such as saunas, cold baths and spas. Its greatest wealth is its tiles which decorated the various parts of the building and which are still visible even today.

Church of São Francisco

Church of São Francisco

Évora, whose historic centre was classified as a World Heritage Site by UNESCO in 1986, is known as the city-museum. This epithet was given to it as it is one of the richest cities in the country in terms of monuments. Its origins date back more than two millennia and its name derives from *Ebora Liberalitas Julia*, the name given to it by the Roman people.

It is a city with imposing churches, historical squares, medieval streets and whitewashed houses. On every corner and every curb side, there is a story to tell. The monument associated with this city is a Roman temple, built in the first century AD and dedicated to the imperial cult and not the Goddess Diana, as is usually mentioned. Near this temple is the Cathedral, which became the largest Portuguese medieval cathedral. It was built in the late thirteenth and early fourteenth century. Its exterior displays towers and buttresses, which demonstrate its defensive role. Inside, you can admire magnificent cloisters, paintings and sculptures.

Some streets below you will come across the *Praça Giraldo* and the Town Hall. *Praça Giraldo*, where much of the trade in the city is concentrated, is a central historical plaza, characterized by its various arcades and a fountain in the centre. At the Town Hall you can visit the ruins of a spa with its public baths from Roman times. You can also admire the work of the architect Francisco Arruda - the *Aqueduto da Água de Prata* – between the *Porta da Lagoa* and the *Porta de Avis*. Originally built to carry water to the *Praça do Giraldo*, the name of this aqueduct is derived from the crystalline waters that it carried from the *Fonte da Prata*.

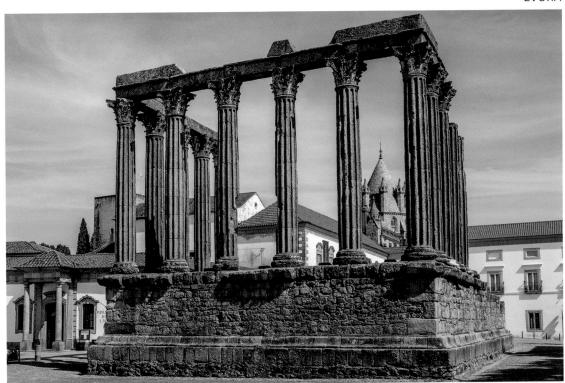

Roman temple

The 15th century **Igeja de São Francisco** is one of the most notable Gothic examples, with its stunning paintings and altars. Another attraction of this church is its chapel, the *Capela dos Ossos*, which has the particularity of having its interior lined with bones from the town's cemeteries. Built in the seventeenth century, the chapel displays a rather intimidating phrase at its entrance "We bones that are here are waiting for yours". This thinking reflects the mind-set of the monks who had the chapel built. The monks decided to remove the skeletons from the earth and use them to build and decorate a chapel. The idea was to convey a message to the population about the transience and fragility of human life. This theory gained momentum during the Baroque period.

The Chapel of Bones, with three naves and lit by small slits, is a monument dedicated to *Senhor dos Passos* or *Senhor Jesus da Casa dos Ossos*.

Chapel of Bones

Chapel of Bones

Praça de Giraldo

In the **Southwest Alentejo Natural Park and Vicentina Coast** we can find cliffs, crags, beaches and reefs, with a mixture of Mediterranean, North Atlantic and African vegetation and several endemic species. This is a great location for bird watching as you can see many birds such as the rare osprey and white storks, which nest in the cliffs. Another rarity are the otters, which can be seen in their natural habitat.

Over the centuries, the population worked in agriculture and fishing, but tourism is increasingly important, especially in places like *Porto Covo* and *Vila Nova de Milfontes*. Among the various activities, highlights include climbing, paragliding, horse riding, canoeing, surfing, scuba diving and golf.

The beaches are much sought after by surfers, as they have the best the waves in the country. You can find long sandy beaches or small beaches nesting between rocks and cliffs, such as in *Porto Covo*, *Malhão*, *Vila Nova de Milfontes*, *Almograve* and *Zambujeira do Mar*. There are many beaches which are still unspoilt.

Zambujeira do Mar

147

Snow in the Algarve

Yesterday I was on the terrace watching the sun gently take its leave of the rocks with an almost imperceptible slowness. I closed my eyes to concentrate on that dialogue which cools the days. I felt someone sit next to me and very unwillingly I opened my eyes and observed the lady who sells the Berliner doughnuts. She asked me if I wanted one. She still had some remaining and at that hour she no longer had the strength for another round of sales along the sand. Looking into her large round open eyes and outstretched hand, I accepted the offer and the company.

I was amazed when she told me that I needed to hear a story and, if I liked it, in return I would have to buy the rest of the cakes. I peeped at the basket and accepted the daring challenge. It was not the first time that I had attracted unexpected conversations, so I let myself travel to when the Algarve was Al-Gharb, and belonged to the Arabs.

In Silves the young Caliph Ibn-Almundim lived, who fell in love with a beautiful Nordic girl, daughter of a great lord, who had been defeated in battle by the Moors. She was called Gilda and, gradually, the Moorish king managed to win her trust and her heart. They married and had a great party. Gilda's smile lit up the nights of the handsome king.

The days went by and with them, Gilda's smile faded until her mouth seemed just a trace of what it had been. The caliph tried all his tricks to get her to smile again, but everything was in vain. So he called on scholars from the different corners of the world. However, no one could find an explanation for the source of that endless grief. One day an old Nordic man was passing by and immediately understood the unusual situation. He explained to the king that Gilda was accustomed to seeing her kingdom covered in snow and missed the whiteness of the fields.

Ibn-Almundim ordered that thousands of almond trees be planted, next to the windows of the palace, until they were lost from sight. Once spring came, the king took Gilda to the window. Her face lightened up when she saw the sea of white petals that had inundated the fields. Every spring, Gilda and her loved one would watch the almond trees come into blossom with huge smiles on their faces.

I bought the rest of the Berliner doughnuts from the lady and, board in hand, I walked off to the sands.

Susana Fonseca

Arrifana Beach

Arrifana Beach panoramic view

Aljezur was founded in the tenth century by the Arabs, who, in addition to bequeathing its name and some legends, left important marks such as the castle and the cistern, The Aljezur municipality forms part of the beautiful Vincentine Coast. Its beaches, enclosed by tall schist cliffs, are a must, especially at the time of the setting sun. It is a paradise for fishermen, surfers, body boarding and nature lovers.

The *Arrifana* beach is surrounded by high cliffs and is great for families during the summer and out of this season it is very popular with water sports enthusiasts who seek it out for its beauty and its waves. At the south end, there is a rock known as the Stone Needle. The Vincentine Coast, where a steep rocky coastline alternates with its coves, stretches to Odeceixe. The Sagres Biogenetic Reserve, located between Cape St. Vincent and the Ponta de Sagres, contains a unique ecological system that attracts zoologists and botanists from all over the world.

Lighthouse of São Vicente

Fortress of Sagres

Fortress of Sagres, Wind Rose

Cabo de Sagres was initially called *Promontorium Sacrum* (the sacred promontory). The location of the fortress, which gives rise to the idea that the earth would end here, has always been the source of many stories, legends and mysteries. This fortress played a historical role during the Age of the Discoveries, when Prince Henry the Navigator had it constructed. Sagres was the last haven for navigators who left in search of new worlds. Inside the fortress you can see some monuments, such as the wind rose, which were found during excavation work, and the *Igreja de Nossa Senhora da Graça*.

Here you can find the tomb of a Spanish captain who helped defend the fortress from the attacks of Sir Francis Drake. Of note is the magnificent view you have from the fortress. This is a magical landscape that transports us into the literary work the *Lusíadas* by Luís de Camões. A few kilometres away, *Cabo de São Vicente* has a lighthouse, which Queen Dona Maria II had built in 1846, with the aim of pointing out potential hazards along the coast. Nowadays this lighthouse, the light of which shines out from a height of 86 metres, watches over one of the busiest trade routes in the world.

Silves main view

Castle of Silves

Cathedral of Silves

Statue of D. Sancho I

Located in the Serra de Monchique, **Silves** is a town steeped in history. Under Muslim rule, it was a large city with several palatial houses. It is a place that makes us dream about movies such as *Aladdin*.

One of the monuments to visit is the Town Hall, which features a neoclassical exterior with its interior in the Neo-Mudéjar style. It is worth noting the glass dome in shades of gold and brown. Beside the Town Hall, alongside the *Torreão da Porta da Cidade*, is located the last of the four Almedian gates.

The castle is situated at the top of the street, built during the rule of the Moors, and this rose up alongside the construction of the walls. You can find traces of the palatial dwellings and an *aljibe*, a large cistern, which is also called the "*Cisterna da Moura*". The name is associated with the legend that tells that on the night of São João you can hear the wailing of a Moorish princess who is waiting on a silver and golden rowing boat for her prince to come and collect her. Be sure to visit the historical centre, with its narrow streets and steep slope.

Dona Ana Beach

Lagos Coastal Road

Lagos, donated by Dom Afonso V to Prince Henry the Navigator, was important during the Age of Discoveries. It was from here that Gil Eanes set off with the aim of rounding Cape Bojador.

You can visit the *São Sebastião* Church and the Castle of the Governors, which was built by the Arabs. According to tradition, it was from the Manueline window that in 1579 Dom Sebastião attended a final Mass before leaving for the battle of Alcácer Quibir. Be sure to go to the various beaches in Lagos, such as *Dona Ana*, the *Pinhão*, *Batata* and *Porto dos Mós*, and take a boat tour and admire the fantastic beaches and the *Ponta da Piedade* headland. And do not forget to take in the caves, the jagged rocks, the crystal clear water and the view.

Prainha Beach

Alemão Beach panoramic view

Portimão, close to the Alvor estuary, is one of the largest cities in the Algarve and historically was an important port. The Mother Church of *Nossa Senhora da Conceição* was built in the fifteenth century and damaged in the 1755 earthquake. Despite the several periods of reconstruction it has undergone, it still retains its Gothic portal. One of the attractions of the town is *Praia da Rocha*, with its long sandy beach surrounded by huge red rocks located within a picturesque setting. Alongside the beach, the marina offers restaurants and shops where you can also discover a heavenly swimming pool. By the marina you can visit the *Fortaleza de Santa Catarina*, built in the seventeenth century to protect the population from attacks by pirates. From the fortress you can take in beautiful views of the extensive beach, the marina and the colourful buildings that surround it.

In August Portimão hosts the Sardine Festival, one of the busiest culinary events in the country,

Outside the centre, it is also worth seeking out the *Praia do Vau* and the *Dunas de Alvor*.

Albufeira Beach

The city's name of **Albufeira** derives from the Arabic *Al-Buhera*, which means *sea castle*, due to the lagoon that was forming in the downtown area. This white-washed fishing town became, from 1960 onwards, one of the most important tourist places in the Algarve. Near the centre you can visit the *Capela da Misericórdia*, which was built in the sixteenth century on the site of a mosque. Another monument that can be visited is the *Torre do Relógio*, located in the former county jail. Considered to be the *ex-libris* of the city, this tower received an iron crown in the nineteenth century, which holds the bell.

Strolling through the streets and alleys with their various grocery shops and souvenir shops, you will come out on to the various beaches - *Pescadores*, *Peneco*, *Túnel* and *Inatel*. At *Peneco* beach, you can take the elevator and enjoy the wonderful panoramic view. Albufeira has no shortage of bars and nightclubs to go out and have fun, and it is also known for its animation on summer nights.

Cathedral

Church of Carmo

It is presumed that **Faro's** origin dates back to a Phoenician trading post, later transformed into the notable Roman city of Ossonoba. In 1031, the city gained its current name thanks to the Arab prince Mohamed Ben Ibne Harun, who founded his independent kingdom here. The *Rua de Santo António* is an open-air commercial hub with beautiful Portuguese cobblestones. At the end of the street you will find the Manuel Bívar garden where, besides the marina, there is a 19th century bandstand. Enter the oldest part of the city through the *Arco da Vila*, opened in 1812. There you will find another arch in the shape of a horseshoe: this is the *Porta Árabe* from the 1st Century. A short climb will take you to the Cathedral, which was built in 1251 on the site of a mosque. Its interior has richly decorated altars and there is also a baroque organ. Outside, you can visit the Chapel of Bones or climb the bell tower and enjoy a beautiful panoramic view over the city. Opposite the church is the Episcopal Palace, a 16th century example of plain architecture.

The walls and the castle have two watchtowers to defend the *Arco do Repouso*.

Episcopal Seminary and the Formosa River in the background

Arco da Vila

Arco do Repouso

Marina of Vilamoura

Oceânico Old Course Golf Course

Vilamoura appeared out of a dream to create one of the largest tourist complexes in Europe. This area was once a rural farming property. Nowadays, in addition to being a haven for golf lovers, the city offers good facilities to practise horse riding, tennis and water sports. Do not miss the nightlife with a trip to the casino, a nightclub or a bar. Vilamoura also boasts a marina, with several pleasant terraces and two blue flag award winning beaches: *Praia da Marina* and *Praia da Rocha Baixinha*.

Near Vilamoura, you can explore the Roman ruins of *Cerro de Vila*, where there is an archaeological site. There you can view the ruins of a noble house or *Villa* and public baths, some fish salting tanks, the foundations of a funerary tower and a port. Some of the tiles found here were the inspiration for the "Vilamoura" brand.

Barril Beach

Tourist Train

Tavira is located on the banks of the river Gilão and is known as "the city of little churches". It was occupied by the Phoenicians, who built a wall on Santa Maria hill, traces of which still remain. Later on, the Muslims transformed the city into one of the most important in the Algarve. From the top of the castle you can enjoy a magnificent panoramic view. Visit the *Igreja de Santa Maria do Castelo*, which is known for its Gothic portal. Another church to visit is the Igreja da Misericórdia, which is considered one of the finest Renaissance examples in the Algarve. Also worth discovering is the historic centre where you can take in the existing Arab traces on each door, window and room.

Tavira is located by the coast, by the islands of Tavira and Cabanas. It has beaches of fine white sand, such as *Terra Estreita*, *Barril* and *Homem Nú*. Access to Barril beach is by a picturesque tourist train. In the coastal area, there are several natural salt marshes, marshlands and dunes, which form part of the Ria Formosa Natural Park.

Sea products occupy a prominent place in its gastronomy, particularly shellfish, octopus, tuna and grilled fish.

Saltpans

EDITORIAL PROJECT:
Objecto Anónimo, Lda.

AUTHORS:
Pedro Veloso, Susana Fonseca, Sérgio Fonseca

GRAPHIC DESIGN / PHOTOGRAPHY:
Pedro Veloso, Sérgio Fonseca, Maria Manuela Morais

TEXT EDITING AND COORDINATION / CREATIVE TEXTS:
Susana Fonseca

TRANSLATION:
David Hardisty, Maria M. F. A. Costa, Susana Santos, Alexandra Andresen Leitão

SPECIAL THANKS TO:
Câmara Municipal do Porto, Casa das Histórias, Casa da Música, Casa de Fados Bacalhau de Molho, Casa de Fados Dragão de Alfama, Casa de Mateus, Caves Calém, EGEAC, Fado ao Centro, Fundação de Serralves, Fundação Mata do Buçaco, Grutas de Mira de Aire, Igreja e Torre dos Clérigos, Instituto dos Vinhos do Douro e Porto, Livraria Lello, Município de Santa Maria da Feira, Museu do Douro, Museu do Fado, Museu Monográfico de Conimbriga, Oceanário, Palácio da Bolsa, Palácio de Vidago, Parques de Sintra - Monte da Lua, Portugal dos Pequenitos, Quinta do Seixo, Quinta do Vesúvio, Quinta Nova de Nossa Senhora do Carmo, Sé Catedral do Porto, Turismo de Lisboa and Universidade de Coimbra.

PHOTOGRAPHY CREDITS:
Coleção do Instituto dos Vinhos do Douro e do Porto, I. P., autoria de Álvaro Cardoso de Azevedo (Casa Alvão), page 25 (1)
Luisa Oliveira, pages 120 (3), 121 (2)
Marco Silva, page 12 (2)
Museu do Douro, page 25 (2)
Shutterstock: Gustavo Frazao, book cover (1); StockPhotosArt, page 94; Damira, page 101 (1); Val Thoermer, page 102 (1); Gilmanshin, page 118 (2)

PICTURE'S DESCRIPTION:
Book Cover: Marinha Beach, Algarve
Tower of Belém - Lisbon, page 1
Rabelo boats and Ribeira- Porto, page 2 and 3
Jerónimos Monastery, Lisboa, page 5

PRINTING:
Norprint.pt

Sixth edition:
July 2018
First Edition - July 2013
© Objecto Anónimo, Lda.

ALSO AVAILABLE IN THE FOLLOWING LANGUAGES:
Portuguese, French, Spanish and German

COLLECTION JOURNEYS AND STORIES (other publications):
Lisbon, Douro Valley, Porto and Northern Portugal, Madeira and Porto Santo

Maia, Portugal
info@objectoanonimo.com
www.objectoanonimo.com

ISBN 978-989-8256-26-3
Depósito Legal 361172/13

Find more books and other products at:

Join us on Facebook feeds and you will be the first to know all the news and activities in Portugal:
www.facebook.com/objectoanonimo